THE ARMOR OF LIGHT

Mandate Series

The Armor of Light

An Anthology of Christian Short Fiction

Merle Meeter, editor
Christian Heritage College

Dordt College Press
Sioux Center, Iowa 51250

Published by Dordt College Press
Sioux Center, IA 51250
Copyright © 1979 by Dordt College Press
Printed and bound in the United States of America

ISBN 0-932914-01-2

AUTHORS

Cor Barendrecht, Joseph Bayly, and Lawrence Dorr are editors as well as imaginative writers.

Paul Borgman, Hugh Cook, Walter Lockwood, Merle Meeter, James Schaap, Mike Vanden Bosch, and Mildred Zylstra are teachers of literature and writing.

Everett L. Huizenga is a corporation lawyer.

Larry Woiwode and E. William Oldenburg (1936-1974) are poets, short-story writers, and novelists.

And Flannery O'Connor (1925-1964) has come to be recognized as one of the foremost writers of our day.

ACKNOWLEDGEMENTS

For permission to reprint materials in this book, the editor is indebted to the following sources.

The Banner for permission to reprint "Not By Dreams Alone" by Cor Barendrecht and "Pink Peppermints" by Mildred Zylstra.

David C. Cook Publishing Co. for permission to reprint "Ceiling Zero" and "I Saw Gooley Fly" by Joseph Bayly copyright © 1973.

For the Time Being for permission to reprint "A Compassion Man" by Walter Lockwood, "Wilbur Finds His Home" by Paul Borgman and "Without a Riderless Horse" by Everett L. Huizenga.

Harcourt Brace Jovanovich for permission to reprint "The Artificial Nigger" by Flannery O'Connor from her volume *A Good Man is Hard to Find and Other Stories* copyright © 1955.

The Reformed Journal for permission to reprint "Lazarus" by Lawrence Dorr copyright © 1973.

Contents

PREFACE

What we need today is realism, we do not deny it, but realism with a vision of hope. We have had enough of gloom, rebellion, purposelessness, and despair. Nor will we be disillusioned again by the fantasies of romanticism heralding a remote perfection. Neither the pastoral naturalism of Steinbeck, nor the stoical posturings of Hemingway, nor the existential cynicism of Camus, Kafka, and Sartre could long satisfy the human search for meaning and happiness. Absurdism, too, has proved febrile and incoherent; no one is content to believe that life is merely a sick cosmic joke.

So now is our opportunity to produce integrally Christian fiction—as well as poetry and drama—by perceiving and objectifying life in the perspective of the Scriptures. As Flannery O'Connor puts it: "The meaning of our life is centered in our redemption by Christ." This truth is not always easy to accept, however, for both man and the creation are under God's curse on sin, and the wages of sin is death. But He who is the Life is Victor over sin and death through His resurrection. Only in the light of the mighty creative and redemptive works of the Sovereign God, as they climax in Jesus Christ, can man see who he is and what he was made for. Only then, by the Holy Spirit, is the renewed man able to put on the armor of light.

Is the Christian writer, then, limited by his Biblical perspective to matters theological and settings ecclesiastical? Not at all; in fact, he is now able to see the coherence of all things in the Redeemer King, and to embody that meaningful coherence in works of literature. Lawrence Dorr wrote of that vocation in this comment on one of his stories: " 'Lazarus' was my witness to the Lord's acting in the twentieth century . . . and when God talks to one Christian, He talks to them all, to all their individual needs."

To that profession of calling I simply add the hope that many readers may pick up this book and see in its everyday realism and its parabolic narrative the narrow road through the waste land, the only freeway that leads to the Father, through the bridging superstructure of the cross and the tunnel of the empty tomb.

—Merle Meeter

THE REMINISCENCE

Many short stories are born in reflection on personal experiences and on those special persons and memorable times in our lives that have shaped our attitudes and even, to some extent, our characters. Through such influences also, God is working all things for the good of those who love Him.

"The White Rabbit" and "Not by Dreams Alone" are artistically formed recollections narrated by young boys (who are now older and more mature). These stories demonstrate the power and warmth of God's love as revealed in family life, and as contrasted with the bloodshed and drunken madness of war and the sin-frozenness of death.

"The Cold in North Dakota" and "Pink Peppermints" are also youth-perspective stories that portray crucial moments in the lives of their principals. In the first, a boy learns that he too is involved in the rejection, torture, and murder of Jesus Christ; but also, wonderfully, he experiences the patient, acceptant love of that Savior through his parents. In the second, an adolescent girl discovers something of the sustaining love of God as it is manifested to her in the grandmother whom she has hitherto either complained about or patronized.

The last two stories in this section are related by older speakers. Even though told in the third person, reminiscence stories usually have an autobiographical freshness and first-person immediacy. "Lazarus" is a richly textured story that illustrates the amazing grace of God, who answers prayer in ways that we cannot predict or comprehend. This story reminds us not to set theological limits on the sovereignty of the Living God who moves more than mountains.

Finally, the grown-up son in "Without a Riderless Horse" looks back on a life of building ever-bigger barns for the puffed-up idols of ambition and vanity. The imminent death of his mother motivates his awareness that God is giving him the opportunity for a last, ultimate choice.

The characters in these stories are real-life persons whom we confront in their openness. That is, they are not paraded before us in their Sunday best. Even God's greatest saints are sinners, by no means completely sanctified in this life. We should be prepared, then, to look at them in their wretchedness and in their righteousness as God Himself views them in Christ. The Christian author, too, needs our acceptance and encouragement as he attempts to tell us the truth about ourselves and this world for the sake of Jesus Christ our Lord and for the glory of His Name.

HUGH COOK

The White Rabbit

The boy knew that his father must have looked funny to the young married men working at the factory. Every day after finishing his paper route the boy would stop his bike at the plant and wait for his father. At 5:30 the whistle on the roof blew with a shrill blast of steam, and a split second later the young men burst from the building, full of banter, combing their hair and lighting cigarettes, silver lunch pails squeezed between elbow and waist. Then they drove off in shiny cars.

Ten minutes later his father appeared, alone, wearing his black beret and a gray striped suit too baggy for church but still too useful during the week for it to be thrown away. Then he mounted his black Dutch bicycle with the black plastic mud flaps encasing the chain and the top half of the rear wheel, and he pedaled the four miles home with the boy.

"How was it today?" the boy's grandfather asked when they got home.

"The same," his father replied. "All we did today was print milk cartons, ten hours of it. Tomorrow we do frozen fish cartons."

"Here you are the best butcher in the country, and all you do is print little paper boxes," his grandfather snorted. "High time it is you left that place, Jaap."

"Ja, I know, but we can't yet."

The boy sensed his grandfather's impatience. Each day that dragged by without bringing to reality Opa's dream of a butcher shop in Canada only increased his misery, and he would sidle aimlessly through the house, muttering pronouncements at anyone or anything he thought needed them:

"Nieko, tie your shoelace! Next thing you know you will your neck break, and then see what kind of a medical bill we would have. Unless the government pays for that too already!"

"Joop, if you are downstairs going anyway, take an empty pail along and fill it with coal when you come back up. That's the trouble nowadays—nobody uses their heads anymore!"

He would sit in his living room chair, listening to phonographs of Psalms sung by a choir of Dutch fishermen. Or he would prop his high black shoes up on a hassock, his chin tilted sharply so that he could read through the bottom part of his bifocals. He spent hours reading the newspapers from Holland, but they only put him in a bad mood, for he saw little happening there of which he approved.

"Hhmmph!" he grunted. "Look at here. *Verdraaid,* if the country isn't turning socialist. Those Nazis were one thing, but it's a good thing we left when we did, Jaap," he said to the boy's father. "Three civil servants for every decent working man. And for everything you need their permission. 'You want to build on your house an addition? Fill out an application. Paint your house yellow? Fill out a form. Remodel your bathroom? Come to our office.' Next thing you know we would need their permission to paint the toilet seat! And if they didn't like the color of my water after I eat beets, a *stommeling* of a civil servant we would have knocking on our door!"

"That's better than to do it by the tree in the back yard like you do now," the boy's mother said.

"Ach woman, what do you know about these things!" he flamed. "Stick to your cooking and your sewing and your silly perfumes!"

The boy noticed his father trying to keep Opa busy by giving him little jobs to do around the house, like painting a room or building a closet, but these chores were not his trade. His hands were clumsy with a brush or a hammer. A knife was another thing. A knife was an extension of his right hand, as if he had been born with one there.

One day the boy's father came home triumphantly with a

white rabbit dangling from his outstretched hand. "Got it cheap from Reitsma," he said, and handed it to Opa. When the boy saw his grandfather head for the basement with the dead rabbit he knew something was about to happen. He followed stealthily and hid in the darkness at the top of the stairs.

He saw Opa string up the rabbit by the hind legs, then take two knives and sharpen them by honing them on each other rapidly, the blades flashing in miniature duel. Opa took one of the knives and made a slit through the fur at each heel, just below the noose. Then he stripped the white pelt off the rabbit just as a person strips off soiled garments, and the sound was like the ripping of cloth.

When Opa was done the boy was shocked by the nakedness of the glossy red body dangling from the ceiling. Stripped of its coat it looked so small that the white fur still on its feet resembled baby bootees, but now grotesquely huge. The boy knew then that he could not eat of the rabbit.

His mother served it next day, with red wine to celebrate the event. She seemed surprised when he mumbled his no thanks.

"But Joop, it's good meat."

Opa did not let him off that easily. "Wait a minute, young man," he said in Dutch. "What do you mean you don't like it. Not good enough it is for you? Do you realize what people would have given for this during the War? Men had their throats slit for less, do you know that?" and he rasped his thumb across his adam's apple. His white hair bristled, his face was red with blood, and the loose flesh beneath his chin shook like the wattles of an old rooster.

At the end of the meal, as the boy's father was about to read the Bible passage, Opa took the Bible from his hand and turned to a different page. Then he looked around the table, and when he was satisfied that all were properly reverent he began to read, and the boy felt the cadence of the phrases as they seemed to rain down in blows upon his head: "O give thanks to the Lord for he is good . . . let the redeemed of the Lord say so . . . he gathered them out of lands . . . they wandered in the wilderness . . . and he delivered them . . . he led them by a straight way . . . let them thank the Lord . . . for he satisfies him who is thirsty, and the hungry he fills with good things."

Later in the evening when his father went to the basement the boy followed and asked him why Opa was always so grouchy. "Things are a bit difficult for Opa right now," his father said, putting his arm around the boy's shoulder. "It's not easy for you to understand, I know, but Opa needs to have something to do, and maybe he felt insulted when you refused to eat the rabbit."

"I didn't mean it that way," the boy said. "Besides, he's grouchy all the time. And he's always talking about the War. Why does he have to talk about the War all the time?"

Then his father told him what had happened to Opa during the War.

He needed to think about that, and he went upstairs. He lay on his bed and thought about what his father had just told him, about the bomb that had struck Opa's house during the War. It had come with a high whistle, and then smashed the house to burning rubble. After the explosion Opa regained consciousness and began to search frantically in the burning ruin for his wife and relatives. He found his wife buried to her shoulders under brick and rock. Minutes later she had died. Then the fire forced Opa out of the ruin, and he could only stand by helplessly. After the blaze had died down, townspeople went in to search for the victims. In one blow the boy's grandmother, three uncles, and three aunts had been killed.

He lay on his back, thinking, and a memory came. He must have been about two. He was playing with wooden blocks on the living room floor when all at once he heard the staccato beat of marching boots on the cobblestones outside, and when he ran to the window and pushed aside the white gauze curtains he saw the soldiers, the German soldiers in the street below, coming right toward him. He peered from just above the window sill, watching the soldiers march closer and closer until they were right below him in the street, the faces hard beneath the rakish helmets, the precise rows of rifles with bayonets pointing upwards, the boots pounding on the cobblestones, the thunderous clack clack clack ricocheting between the high brick buildings in the narrow street, then echoing in his ears like a snare drum, and he dropped beneath the window sill in fright and closed his eyes tight and clamped his hands over his ears, but still he heard the boots, as if he were in a bad dream with a train hurtling toward him without his being able to move, the train shrieking by at the last minute, the vibration pounding through his whole body, until the metal rhythm had receded. Finally he rose. The soldiers were gone.

He brooded over these things and felt again his fear of that time, so that he felt suddenly cold. And then he thought he began to understand a little bit better why Opa was the way he was. But with the understanding came revulsion, for his grandfather's world seemed at that moment to be made of blood.

His father's servitude to Laban, as Opa often put it, did not last seven years. After three years in the factory, his father was able to buy a store on the main street of the south Ontario town in which they lived.

On a raw day in late November they moved. All that day they hauled furniture and boxes out of the old house and moved them into the living quarters above the store—even Opa carried whatever he could. The boy's mother kept telling him not to strain himself, to carry lighter objects, and please! to wear a scarf, but Opa shrugged her off: "*Ach, Kind,* why don't you pack the kitchen things. We men will worry about the rest," he said, coughing as he helped guide the heavy pump organ onto the truck.

By mid-December the store was ready. Opa watched the painter put the finishing touches on the sign in the window: "Witte's Meats," the white letters painted in an arc just as they had been on the store window in Amsterdam.

The front of the store was brightly lit and often there was laughter, the boy's father presiding over the business with a ready wink in his eye. He would tell stories when the ladies of the congregation came in, for he was happy, and so were the women to have a Dutch butcher in town. They would hold a hand to their mouths as they laughed, self-consciously hiding the ill-colored caramel gums of their dentures.

"Sausage just as you like it from the old country," the boy's father would say, "with not too much garlic in it!"

Opa, too, was a different man, and the boy sensed it as he

watched him in back of the store. Opa did most of the actual butchering, taking the large pieces of meat that came from the packers and cutting them down to steaks, roasts, and chops.

The boy was both attracted and repelled by those huge slabs of meat carried into the dusky cutting room. He felt about the meat as he did about touching his tongue to a frozen bridge railing on the way to school: he knew the disastrous results of making contact, yet was inescapably drawn to do so. There was something both repulsive and magnetic about the huge carcasses hanging stiffly from the gleaming metal hooks in the cooler, red meat flecked with white fat, the purple liver, heart, and tongue dangling from the neck at the bottom. A pork chop lying under the front counter's stark fluorescent lights was one thing, but the meat carcasses hanging in the macabre light of the cooler resembled their former state closely enough to rouse fear in the boy. The smell of blood hung coldly in the air.

One day the boy stood in the cutting room watching Opa dress some meat, his frock so splotched with deep red blood it looked as if it had been washed in it. His accurate arm raised the cleaver and brought it down thwok! through a bone and onto the carving block. Then he went to the front.

The boy approached the block, drawn to the slab of red meat. White sinews ran through it like a river on a map, thin streams radiating from the main one. He brought his forefinger to touch the meat, and was surprised by its softness and wetness. As he drew his hand away he saw the blood on his finger. He looked for a place to wipe it, not wanting to clean it on his pants, but there was no rag in the room. He turned his finger along the side of the carving block and left a thin, snaky line. He looked at the cleaver, tried to lift it by the handle, and found it unexpectedly heavy. He rasped his thumb lightly across the sharp edge, then quickly withdrew his hand when he felt the keenness of the blade over each thin line of his thumbprint.

Then Opa returned, adjusted the meat on the block, and began cutting out the fat, the thin knife slicing easily through the meat. His hands were covered with blood, and moved deftly, without wasted motion. Then he took the meat to the front of the store, placed it in trays under the glass counter, and stepped into the cooler for another piece of meat.

He emerged cradling a slab of pork in his arms. When the huge door closed behind him with a heavy click, the boy imagined what it would be like locked in the cooler; he saw himself pounding on the door, screaming to be freed from his dark and cold imprisonment with those hulking corpses.

Opa began sharpening his knives, just as he had done before skinning the rabbit, and the boy saw again the stripping of the pelt that was just like the sound of ripping cloth.

"Are you going to be a butcher when you grow up, Joop?" Opa asked him in Dutch.

He had not expected the question, and was unsure of just how much lay behind it. He was the oldest son. How much had been decided for him?

"No, Opa," he said.

"Why not?"

"I don't know. Don't like it, I guess."

"What will you be then?"

He did not know what to say. He felt only a desire, still chaotic, for a cleaner world than that of his grandfather, a world of order and light and no blood.

He shrugged his shoulders.

"But you *something* have to be," Opa said.

Then the boy felt the blood rising to his cheeks, and he blurted, "Well, I'm not going to be a butcher, that's for sure! That's all you do—cut up dead animals!" and what he expected then was a cuff on the head, as if he had said something profane.

But he felt his grandfather's heavy hand, covered with dried blood, resting on his head, and he heard, "That's all right, *m' jongen*. There's no hurry. But in the meantime, throw these pieces of fat into that pail over there, will you?"

The boy looked up at his grandfather from beneath the heavy hand. Opa seemed serious.

He gathered the pieces of fat into his hand, threw them into the pail, and ran upstairs. There he washed his hands.

The boy's bedroom was up in the third story of the house, and he was fond of looking out the window at the people on the sidewalk across the street far below. Especially that winter he felt warm and safe there high in his heaven.

He watched the white snow settle on the pavement. Smoke drifted from the chimneys across the street. He placed his cheek against the cold window and looked up to see the flakes, wondering where so many could possibly come from. When he looked down at the snow against the red brick storefronts the flakes were white and they drifted lazily down, but when he looked up into the sky they were dark and they swirled angrily about.

That particular Christmas they had much to celebrate, what with the opening of the store. The spruce tree stood high, its silver peak reaching the ceiling. They had decorated the tree all together, sprinkling tinsel through the branches and hanging ornaments and colored balls, and when his mother lit the candles in the room, the glow reflecting in the many ornaments, it seemed to him the tree contained a thousand candles.

His mother baked almond ring and *gevulde koek* and iced mocha tarts, and when some friends from the congregation came for the day, the men smoking fat Dutch cigars and drinking red wine, the room hung heavy with a pall of cigar smoke, and the smell of wine filled the house as it does in church during Communion.

That evening he held his father's hand as they walked through the softly falling snow to church. His grandfather coughed again, and his mother said, "Opa, you should have worn your scarf," and he said to her, "Can't a man have a little cough nowadays?" In church, the many flickering candles made him drowsy so that he fell asleep, the soft notes of *Stille Nacht, Heilige Nacht* drifting into his ears as his head nodded and then fell against his father's arm.

Three days later the boy did not see his grandfather in the store. "Opa's not feeling well," his mother said, but he saw in her eyes the wild look of a small animal in fear.

That night he could not fall asleep. He left his door open and saw his mother running in and out of Opa's room next to his with a hot water bottle or a glass of hot anise milk. Finally he fell into a fitful sleep.

In the middle of the night he awoke and heard a voice feebly singing, and it was some time before he recognized the voice as Opa's. His grandfather was singing Dutch Psalms.

The boy lay there in the dark suddenly awake, transfixed by the scratchy voice singing slightly off key. The voice pulled him out of bed, for he felt it as the prelude to some revelation. He tiptoed stealthily through the darkness to the next door. It stood ajar. He peeked into the room and saw his father with his back to him, standing by Opa's bed, holding Opa's hand. They did not see him, although he felt certain they would hear the pounding of the blood at his temples.

Opa lay propped against white pillows. He was dressed in a nightshirt white as the snow. His eyes were closed, and his head with its shock of white hair rolled slightly to and fro according to the rhythm of the thin melody escaping from his bloodless lips.

Then his grandfather began to sing a song familiar to the boy, for he had heard it in church that Christmas:

> Now may thy servant, Lord,
> According to thy word,
> Depart in exultation.

Opa finished the song in tremulous voice, the last frail notes seeming to hang frozen in the air.

The boy tiptoed back to his room. He climbed into bed and pulled the blankets over his head, for he felt he had seen a terrible beauty. And all he heard, over and over again, was the sound of the ripping of cloth, until it faded under the stronger echo of his grandfather's song.

Questions for Reflection and Discussion:

1. Why is the grandfather always so angry and irritable in the first half of the story?
2. What does the white rabbit mean to Opa? To the boy?
3. What imagery—similes and metaphors—are especially appropriate and effective?
4. What is the function of the flashback on the German soldiers?

5. Why do you think the boy feels such revulsion for the meat-cutter's trade?
6. In the paragraph just before Opa sings his final song, what is the significance of all the white imagery?
7. In the last sentence, what is the symbolically suggested relationship between the sound of ripping cloth and the grandfather's song?

COR BARENDRECHT

Not By Dreams Alone

Pa already had asked Rein to go outside to get more wood from the shed. But the boy was sitting on the coconut rug next to the woodstove, watching the blue flames dancing on the logs and daydreaming. His legs wrapped in an old army blanket, he thought of himself as a knight sitting near an open fire in a castle.

A minstrel from Italy had come to visit the castle to entertain the household during the cold winter. The minstrel had traveled long distances on foot. He entertained the knight with stories of pilgrimages and wars. At the moment Pa called, the minstrel was almost finished telling about Jacques de Bourbon, the king of Naples. The king had met a saint and was so impressed by the words he'd heard that he had shed his royal robe and put on sackcloth tied around the waist with a cord.

The minstrel had followed the king from village to village. The king would ride into the towns sitting in a dung barrow, practicing humility. He was followed by courtiers dressed in the colorful clothes of the aristocracy. The courtiers were proud and sought honor for themselves. Rein thought he heard the rumble of a wheelbarrow outside, but then realized that the heavy snow would muffle the sound.

"It's getting dark and the fire is dying down," Pa said.. "You'd better get that wood right now."

"Yes, Pa," Rein said. He stood up and stretched himself. Slowly he walked to the coat rack, took his winter coat, and put on his gloves. Brr! it really was cold! He pulled the woolen scarf over his head and walked toward the shed. When he got there, he found the door frozen shut. He went back into the house, asked for a crowbar, and again outside in the snow, he pried the door open.

In the shed he gathered an armful of chopped wood. Knights probably keep their pajamas on under their clothes in wintertime, he thought. He'd kept his on all week. Ma hadn't complained, because this was the coldest winter the Netherlands had seen in a century. The ice in the streams and rivers was two feet thick. Transport trucks crossed the river on the ice. People were freezing to death alongside the roads. Schools had been closed, streetcars had stopped running, and food deliveries discontinued. And it was only December. The temperature had not been much above zero all month. No change was foreseen. Rein stamped the snow off his shoes at the back door.

"Only a bushel left, Pa," he said as he handed the wood to his father.

"Thank you. We'll have enough to last us until the morning. Then we'll see about getting some more." Rein knew Pa was trying to be casual about the lack of fuel. Pa really would be thinking about the wood all night. The few trees that had grown in the small city backyard had been chopped down and used for fuel earlier in the cold winter. The nearby woods were occupied by German soldiers who had built bunkers and a fifteen foot deep anti-tank ditch around the area. The small coal supply from the Limburg mines had been claimed by the enemy for use in the gin industry and in army quarters. The supply of coal from Wales had stopped at the beginning of the war when seaports had been closed. Pa wouldn't watch the fire die without agonizing about where to get more wood.

"Maybe Uncle Joe can help. Doesn't he have fuel for his bakery?"

"We'll ask Uncle Joe tomorrow, after Christmas," Pa said with finality. He picked out some pieces of wood from the bundle, lifted the pan rings from the top of the stove and lowered the fresh wood into the fire.

It had grown darker. Ma, who had sat near the window darning socks, stood up to close the red velour curtains. They'd keep the heat inside and also prevent the little light coming from an oil wick set in a glass of water from shining out the window. Ma didn't like to eat in public. It would make people who didn't have anything to eat jealous, she thought.

On her way to the kitchen she said, "Clara, please bring some chairs around the table; I'm going to dish up the food." Rein's younger sister, who had been writing a letter, did as she was told. It was a strange Christmas day. Of the ten children, only the two of them were home. Their brothers and sisters were staying with farmers who exchanged food for work.

Clara and Rein had walked to church with Pa and Ma, holding on to them to keep them from sliding on the ice under freshly fallen snow. They'd come to the unheated gymnasium where services were held. They had kept on their coats in church. The dominie had walked in exactly on time, preceded by elders and deacons dressed in black. The congregation had risen. "Out of respect for the Word and the office," Pa had explained once when Rein had asked why.

The dominie began, "Our help is in the name of the Lord."

"It's called the *votum*," Pa whispered. "It means that this isn't a town hall meeting, but a church stating its declaration of dependence," he continued needlessly. Rein thought there must be other differences too, like "grace, peace, and mercy" that were to be multiplied. After church he'd ask Pa by what factor.

The organ played the Christmas anthem *"Ere Zij God"* and the people followed, singing "Glory to God in the highest, and on earth peace, good will toward men" eleven times and ending with two long, drawn-out amens. During the singing Rein would have given something precious from his pocket—an old coin, even his best marble—to be one of the shepherds, to watch the angels, and to run down to the stable in the village and see the Christ in a feeding trough. He could almost smell hay and dung when he thought of it. A droning voice coming from the pulpit reminded him that admission to that stable was by faith. The sobering Christmas sermon shattered his dreams about shepherds and angels. After the service they'd walked home in a blistering snowstorm. They'd sat around and read books and talked about who'd been missed in church.

When the table was ready, Ma brought in the rabbit on a dish. The rabbit had been kept in a cage in the back yard. It was a big white Albino with red eyes, that weighed thirteen pounds clean. Pa stood up to say the prayer that always was the same. But today the words seemed to have a different tone. Pa asked for a blessing on the rabbit and for peace and warmth for the family. Rein's mouth began watering.

As Pa prayed, he looked at the rabbit through his eyelashes. The smell of broiled meat rose to his nostrils. It made him think of white rabbits as big as clouds in the sky. He played with the rabbits and leaped with them over the blue rivers that ran between the clouds. When you get hungry, Rein thought, you just catch a rabbit and you eat and eat until you're so full you can hardly walk. Clara elbowed him, because he was staring at the rabbit with his hands folded, and Pa, who was done praying, looked at him.

"You want the head, son?"

"Yes, please! Can I keep it and put it on the shelf above my bed?"

"We'll see. You have to get the meat off first." Rein worked around the jawbones and inside the skull of the rabbit with a sharp knife until the head was clean. He'd ask Ma if he could boil the rest of the meat off the bone. Then he'd reassemble the head and put it on the shelf for show.

When they were done eating, they sang Christmas songs and Pa read Luke 2. He could almost recite the passage without looking in the Bible. When he had finished reading, Ma had a surprise. She had saved the Christmas issue of the Christian monthly that always carried a special story. She asked Pa to read the story. In the story it was always cold, and on Christmas day people usually got a present they had always wanted but didn't dare hope for. They'd suddenly feel warm inside because of the gift.

Pa read well. When the gift came, Ma winked away a tear. Without the story, her Christmas wouldn't have been complete. Rein asked for another story, but Ma said it was enough and time to go to bed. That was the end of Christmas day.

Rein said goodnight. He stopped in the hall to pick up Pa's winter coat from the rack. He took the coat to his bedroom and placed it on the bed as an extra blanket. Without taking off his clothes he slipped into bed. Under the blankets he had his eyes closed and listened to indistinct footsteps thumping and slipping in the snow and to sounds of far-off voices coming nearer. The voices were singing but he couldn't hear any words. Aroused by the sounds, he opened his eyes, jumped out of bed and walked to the window. Carefully he opened a slit of the curtain.

Shadows moved in front of the window. Startled, he saw two drunken soldiers stalking down the snow-covered sidewalk. They sang *"Stille Nacht, Heilige Nacht'"* stopping to hiccough after every word. The soldiers' arms were around each other's shoulders. Guns dangled across their backs. They were getting dangerously close to the unlit lantern post in front of the window. One of them touched the post. He hugged the post as if it were an old friend. Suddenly he grew angry when he felt the post was cold and hard. He grasped his gun, aimed, and pulled the trigger.

The gun went off with a blast. A window shattered across the street. *"Schweinhund!"* the soldier scolded. His comrade laughed and then they both broke into a loud, hollow laughter. They continued singing, *"Alles schlaft, einsam wacht,* ha-ha-ha."

Rein didn't dare move from his place for fear the soldiers would see the curtain wave and shoot in blind drunkenness. He felt relieved when they finally moved on, slipping in the snow until they were out of sight. When the noises faded, he crawled back under the blankets and thought. The soldiers were young, maybe seventeen or eighteen. Maybe they were scared too, or lonely. He remembered how he'd seen homesick soldiers sit around a tall Christmas tree in a restaurant. The tree was decorated with painted, hand-carved ornaments and real white candles. The soldiers just sat around drinking beer. They laughed and were noisy, but some looked sad and sat quietly staring at the flames.

Rein shivered. Even under the covers it was cold. He pulled the blankets over his head and soon dozed into a restless dream. In his dream he saw boys and girls and grown-ups dressed in colorful clothes. They were pushing a dung barrow into the dark city street. In the barrow he saw a child, like a king, wrapped in sackcloth.

Questions for Reflection and Discussion:

1. How does the introductory story of the minstrel and the king relate to what follows?
2. How do Rein's thoughts during the sermon parallel the opening scene of the story?
3. Does his mother's Christmas story have any special significance?
4. Note the number of references to cold and warmth. Which seem particularly meaningful?
5. What is the importance of the drunken-soldiers' scene near the end of the story?
6. Relate Rein's last dream to his first.
7. What is the meaning of the title?

LARRY WOIWODE

The Cold in North Dakota

In North Dakota the first thick-foot freeze often came before Halloween, and with the first heavy snow the world of our countryside was turned upside down. All the color was in the sky. I wanted to walk there the way I walked the fields and streets and byways of packed dirt in distant season, like my uncle who walked on his hands, but that wasn't the same, quite. I wanted to crawl across the curling clouds the way insects and flies crawled across our ceiling.

"Just be happy you're a boy," my father said.

The snow deepened and drifted and then on an afternoon when most of the county schools had been called off, including the one where our father worked, as my brother and I were getting into our bulky clothes to go to the farmhouse at the edge of town, Bendemeer's, to get our daily quarts of milk, he'd walk in to the kitchen and say, "You boys wait," and take down his long brown canvas coat, lined with fleecy sheepskin, put it on over his suit jacket, pull on his floppily buckled overshoes, his cap with furry earflaps that tied, his mittens and gloves, turn up the collar of the coat so it rainbowed above his cap, check and adjust us again, and then say, "All right, now let's go."

The air was so white we couldn't see the hedge around the house, or, after we'd walked a ways, the house itself. An unbound sheet went plunging and groaning around us, and only when the wind blew it off to one side and made it seem the ground had slipped under our feet, only then were we aware of the snow—spiraling at our eyes, over our foreheads, tautening the skin there and turning it numb, dripping from eyelashes, and gathering in powdery lines along the scarves he tied under our eyes with *his* eye on our shrinking well-beings; without them, a gust of this wind turning a corner could make you gag, and that could lead to coughing, which could lead, through the throat and chest diseases, down to a room in the closest hospital, or worse, as I'd learned; and though the wool folds of the scarves smelled like wet dogs and sprouted bristles where our nostrils and mouths were galaxied and gasping behind, putting me in mind of monsters I imagined, they did the job.

"It looks like this is going to be a real blizzard," he said, and dragged his feet to plow the snow aside and blaze a path that we could navigate knee-deep, while we floundered in his wake, protected from the worst of the noise and swirl of it, and held the tails of his coat to keep in touch with his direction through this wind-blown afternoon that had become half night. By the time the gray buildings of Bendemeer's uprose above the blowing sheets, the bristles on our scarves were icicles, and our boots went squeaking over the frozen linoleum of their back porch, all of us panting in the small space, up to our quarts of milk. Columns of white pushed above the tops of their bottlenecks, lifting the printed paper caps up with them, and were like three tipped tophats in a row, seen from the inside. He took the empties from a milk carrier he'd fashioned for us out of a bargained-for orange crate, dropped the full ones into their rack of wood sockets, and with a backhand of his mitten sent the tophats whirligiging off into the mingling whitenesses.

"Let's get back before this gets worse," he said.

If this or a blizzard like it kept up, the roads were soon smothered and blocked, and in the middle of the morning-half of school a team of sleek horses would appear at the end of the street, pulling a hayrack mounted on sleigh runners hewn from wood beams. The bearded driver was wrapped in horse blankets to his fur hat, and balanced himself with a foot against the mast of the rack's front upright, on a heaped load of golden threshing straw. Its glinting mound halted at the schoolhouse doors, the horses nodding at the reins and blowing frost from their heads, and then began to tremble as faces and hands appeared to those of us who looked on from the basement windows cut into diamonds with protective, metal-wire mesh. Our classmates dug caves to keep warm on the trip to town, they said, and the rest of the day were scratching themselves and picking straw out of their clothes.

And when the day outdoors was turning deep blue, the horses would appear outside again, stomping and filligreeing the air with their steam, and there wasn't one classmate I held as a friend, it seemed, who didn't run out and do a disappearing dive into the straw. And then the golden load of it murmured out of town with the secrets children always share at that hour. "I wouldn't care if I froze, if I could ride home in a hayrack once," I said to my brother, as we watched it diminish along the fence-lines of the white-frozen plain.

"Just be happy you live in town," he said.

The parochial school was across the street from us, a pair of snowdrifts away, and on the worst of the winter mornings he and I were the only ones there, other than The Sisters of the Presentation Order, who taught us. It was his second and my first year. I'd poke my finger into the jelly of the hectograph and see if printing came up on it purple blue. Or stick my tongue against the diamond mesh outside and try to pull it loose without losing a ribbon of skin. Or peek from sneaky angles in the Sisters' wimples to see if they really had hair (and what *hue?*) under that shinily pressed white band with its flying black hood. Or listen to the youngest of them tell stories — as she gripped the big beads of her belted rosary in the lap of her floor-length skirt — about boys who'd displeased God by disobeying their parents, teasing animals, or receiving First Communion in a state of mortal sin, and how they were then struck by lightning, she whispered, or evaporated up out of their yards.

Or we scattered seeds and crumbs she gave us over the snowbanks for birds, wiped and washed the classroom slates, cleaned the erasers on a revolving brush in the German janitor's diabolical boiler room, emptied the pencil sharpeners and scraped Crayola shavings from their metal spirals that chewed up wax and wood, and had our fifth piano lesson that week. And then the Sisters, black fluttering birds themselves, had us kneel with them on the floor of the chapel-auditorium as they prayed for the safety of those who weren't with us this gathering, and for fairer weather for the remainder. They helped us on with our sweaters and scarves and coats, smelling of hand cream and the pink medicinal soap they passed out to their classes twice a year, and the scent of their touch clung to us through the towering whiteness to the warmth of our home.

We'd moved into a new house that year. Most of the upstairs was a maze of boxes and unpainted walls, but there *was* an up-stairs, with three rooms and an attic, besides all of the finished rooms on the ground floor that we lived in, and so much space we all felt freer, but all more alone. Privacy. It had a bathroom, too, the first one we'd had, and I didn't miss one bit those icy midnight runs to the outhouse, shanty, biff, or cold pots on the nipping porch; I'd had whooping cough, galloping pneumonia, tonsilitis two winters ago, strep throat and tonsilitis again last fall, and, finally, this winter, my tonsils out.

My brother and I sat at our bedroom window and stared out at the snow.

"Let's get out the sled and go sliding," I said.

"Don't be stupid. That klunker'd sink three feet in this stuff."

"Where's the hedge?"

"Underneath all this. Where do you think?"

"Maybe it went away south."

"Dummy, it has *roots* in the ground. It stays there."

"Is it dead, then?"

"Probably it's hibernating."

"Did Jack Frost do that?" I asked, and scratched the spikes of ice fringing our windowpane.

"There's no such thing as Jack Frost."

I told him the storytelling Sister said that Jack Frost was an elf who had a red suit like Santa Claus, and icicles hanging from his nose. I left some cookies out for him one night, I said, and in the morning they were gone. "There was water there."

"Dad ate them."

I pushed him in the chest and we scuffled around, fell on the bed, and started heading toward the region of homicide.

"Stop that!" a voice cried, and our mother appeared in the door in a flash, flushed to her flying hairline. She brushed back a blackish swirl. "How many times have I told you two how *angry* it makes me to see you fight? Shame on you! Both of You! It's wrong, and you know it; it's a sin! It's even worse when a pair of brothers engage in it. Oh, *you*!"

"Well, he hit me," I said. "When I was just—"

"We weren't really actually fighting," my brother said. "We were ah—practicing double tumbles on the mattresses." He hung his head.

"Forbidden," she said. "Also, you know if you lie to your mother at this time of year, Santa might hear of it." The hooftaps on the housetop. "He has spies."

We both understood this, and fell back on the bed and started moaning and rolling around on the covers.

And now that she'd been our mother, she became herself. "It's stopped snowing," she said. "Did you see?"

"Yes! Yes!" we said, and went to the window.

"Isn't it lovely to be in? Well now anyway. When it was coming down, it was like brooms across the ceiling!"

"It'll be great for sledding," my brother said.

"Yes," she said. "Why don't you two get out in it and enjoy it?"

"Well, if we went out in it now," I said, "that klunker'd sink three—"

"Hey, I just told him that and now *he's* saying it. Tell him to stop! Tell him to quit being so — quite so obstinate!"

This was a word she sometimes used to reprimand us, and hearing it come at me now as it did in his voice dimmed my vision with unbrotherly black-and-blue thoughts.

"And now we're back to where we started to begin with," she said. *"No fighting."*

And having hung that in the air before us, like a coat on a hook, she disappeared.

We dressed and went outdoors. He waded ahead, holding his elbows high, and I watched a wide halo tremble around him as he moved with the telltale plunges of people who moved through my dreams. He stopped at a snowdrift taller than our father and turned to me. We stared at one another over our scarves. Then the big bare tree in the corner of the yard, with its black limbs branching out over us, cracked, and a handful of ice came scattering down on our red-and-blue sledding caps.

"Are you afraid?" he asked.

"Yes," I said. For I was sure, as the Sisters told us, sometimes in warning, that God and Jesus and Mary and the angels were watching over everything all of us ever said and did, and one of them just might decide to appear.

"Maybe God's underneath all this," I said, "Let's dig Him up."

"Don't be stupid," my brother said, and jerked a fuzzy thumb straight up. "He's there."

"Let's dig a cave, then, and hide in it."

"You can't until the crust freezes."

"Let's make a snowman, then."

"You can't until the snow packs, goon."

"Well, what can we do?"

"Go inside," he said.

I struggled over to a white swelling across the yard, dragged myself up on top of it, got my feet underneath me, felt my legs tremble on the trembling, hidden, insubstantial hedge, and then threw out my arms and dove. Dove into a crystalline darkness that supported me. I could fall forever through its enveloping folds. I felt afloat.

"How is it?" my brother called.

"Better than the lake," I cried, and pulled myself out of the glittery grave into sunlight. "Try it and see!"

He did, I did it again, we did it together, and when the snow that was packed into our overshoes and around our collars and cuffs had melted, and then started to freeze again, we finally ran for the house, leaving ragged slashes filled with shadow along the hedge, as though dozens of us had been diving and the sum of our exaltation was preserved by the cold and yielding North Dakota snow.

That night, when I was sure everybody else was asleep, I got out of bed and went to the window. Jack Frost? The yard was silvered by a gold-colored moon, and then the light at the neighbor's went off, closing them behind a blank wall, and the wind came up. It blew along the side of the house and broke in waves on the wing of our bedroom, making the storm windows and the panes in front of me hum with an animal sound that other parts of the house seemed to pick up.

I didn't know what time it was when I woke, and hardly felt the throbbing above my eye; the window was printed with polar flowers, plumes, and frosty continents, except for where my forehead had rested. That spot had been left untouched, or so I reasoned, to keep from waking me up. I dove under covers, into the warm cave my brother made, and rode home in hayracks of snow.

The next day was Christmas Eve. My brother and I dressed in our burdensome clothes and took the crate toward Bendemeer's. Before we got to the football field at the edge of town, we heard hooves on the road behind us, and then a team of horses came jogging up, pulling a shed, almost like an outhouse, mounted on sleigh runners of wood. There was a glass window at the front, and below the window a thin slit for the double reins. A stovepipe stood above its shingled roof and trailed a loose sleeve of smoke across the sky. These rigs replaced the hayracks, now that real winter was here, and I'd heard from my friends how the stoves inside that burned coal and wood and kept them warmer than the furnace at school, or so they claimed, were perfect for popping popcorn on during the long ride in from their farms. They sometimes rode for hours, they said. The red-faced farmer had probably picked up presents for some of them in town.

The horses passed us and cut along the white-wooden goalposts arching over victories of an almost-unremembered season, bringing the sled skimming around behind them, their hooves muffled now in drifts, their backs steaming through the burlap packed under their harnesses for warmth, and headed toward the sun that stained the fields and pastures and scattered clumps of trees across the plain, for as far as we could see on the encircling horizon, orange-golden.

"I wish it was winter all the time," I said.

"If it was, the farmers couldn't raise crops and we'd starve; 'd be the end of it."

"Well, I wish it was Christmas more often."

"Christmas is when Jesus Christ was born."

"I know that."

"Well, we've each got only one birthday, my dear."

I said that Jesus could do or have whatever He wanted, because He was God, but my brother said He couldn't; that's why He died on the cross, he said.

"That's another God," I said. "There are three of them."

"I see you haven't been paying attention in catechism again, dunce hound."

"No sir! I mean, I have too!"

"Then you know He was crucified."

"He was not!"

"Yes He was."

"How come?"

"What do you mean, 'How come?' " he said, in a way of mimicking me that made me feel my zipper was unzipped. "That's what the Bible says."

"Bull-loney!"

"He died for our sins."

"He didn't die for mine!"

"Bull-loney."

"I've never sinned."

"If you haven't, don't worry. You will."

He went toward Bendemeer's, singing Christmas carols as he went, and his breath made gray bells in the air that his high voice rang within. It didn't seem possible that the Christ Child was the crowned and bony, bleeding man nailed to the crucifix above our bedroom door.

My brother got our three quarts of milk, and I let him carry them alone.

A block from the house, I saw our father come out the side porch and took off on a run. He was at the back of the car when I got to him, trying to get an old Army blanket on or off a brown paper-wrapped box in the trunk. He whirled in surprise, and blue smoke fumed around his face and earflaps as he deliberated. Then he said my brother was right.

"Then why have Christmas, Dad? Why pretend it's fun?"

"We rejoice that Jesus, who was the Son of God and also God Himself—a member of the Trinity, of course—came to earth as Man, to be the Savior of us men here."

I heard my brother come on a clattering run with the milk, and the trunk lid slammed down in a frozen rush.

I went inside to see my mother. She'd been brought up in another church, I knew, and had her own ideas about religion and God; she was at the kitchen stove stirring syrup that was about to candy, so she couldn't stop and talk, she said, but as I tugged my way out of my chrysalis of clothes, she told me that Jesus, who was born with the animals and shepherds around Him, did indeed die on the cross. "But that's a reason to celebrate," she said. "Look at His precepts."

So there, I thought.

I went to bed early that Eve of The Night. My brother soon followed, wearing long wool socks over his cold-prone feet, and started whispering under the covers about the box in the trunk, which he was sure held a sled: it was the right size, he whispered; if it was a long sled, and if we each had our own this winter we wouldn't have to take turns all the time, or do those breath-crushing bellyflops across each other's backs. He was speculating about styles and sizes when his whisper dimmed and the regular sound of his breathing drew him into sleep.

I heard singing and went to the window. Loudspeakers had been hung outside the church a block away, and the choir was singing Christmas hymns into a microphone; they'd sing until midnight mass. Their voices spread a silver substance, heavier than the snow, it seemed, over my senses, and the confined area my sight controlled.

It came up-po-on a mid-night clear,
That glorious so-ong of old . . .

I whispered along with them as I stared out at our white lawn in the light of the street lamp.

Away in a manger, no crib for His bed,
The lit-tle Lord Jesus lay down His sweet head . . .

I was positive I wasn't one of the ones who caused Him to die. I didn't even know He was dead. But my mother, too, said everybody was responsible. On His birthday, did they forget?

Joy to the world! the Lord is come!
Let Earth receive her King!

Cold rose from the floor and I couldn't hear singing. If that had happened to Jesus, then what would become of me, a dreamy, sinful child from an unheard-of village in a rural vastness on this whirling world? The wind came up and a lightning-rod cable at the corner of the house slapped against the siding in the cold air, and then the street lamp started to swing, tilting its light over the snowbanks, and there was a sound at the window. The wind, the sudden snowflakes tapping there, were asking to touch me.

I went into the living room. The Christmas lights and the shimmer of the tree in the alcove of the bay window filled the air with the firelight of many-colored, interchanging beams. I thought I heard voices, and then felt such a hush of interior silence I was sure I'd imagined them. I went to the tree and there, beside the mound of packages I'd watched accumulate over a month, was an addition smelling of varnish and runners painted red. My brother was right, again. A new sled. A *Flexible Flyer*, long enough to hold an adult lying flat, or seat three my size. Three.

Farther over, beneath the boughs at the center of the tree, overlaid with a host of different colors, was the Bethlehem scene, spread out and arranged on cotton rolls. The Night Visitors. The camels, cattle, and lambs. The stable with Mary and Joseph in shadow. The Infant on straw with His arms outstretched I imagined layers of flakes like lace curtains unrolled, coulees of snow folding into one another, cold bells ringing their insides across the frigid air, crystals that rose from the landscape and glowed above it in silver dots.

The tree lights guttered around my vision and rainbows swam. I couldn't understand it. Why Him? It wasn't fair to any of us. It was a crime!

I went into the kitchen and looked up at the row of coats on the rack above the oil heater, and decided I might as well start getting dressed up to go out into the cold.

"Say! What do you think you're doing?"

The bulk of my father was dark in the doorway, with the light from the living room shining around behind him.

"I don't know."

"Are you all right?"

"Yes," I said. "I guess."

He came and put a hand over my forehead. "Mmmm," he said. "You're probably still troubled or worried, or whatever, over what you asked today."

"Yes," I said.

"You needn't worry about anybody as willing as He was to accept His station in life. If He did complain, it wasn't more than once. That's a happy man."

I felt myself rise above his shoulders, and then his hands and arms as he gathered me in, then the stride of his feet underneath me, and started thinking about Christmas morning, the gifts under the tree, the new sled, and had just enough time before I reached the bottom of sleep in that North Dakota night, in the warmth of the wide white bed where he tucked me in closer to my brother, to thank Jesus for my father.

Questions for Reflection and Discussion:

1. Why is the third paragraph of this story all one sentence?
2. Which descriptive words and phrases in paragraph five—which begins, "It looks like this is going to be a real blizzard"—do you consider particularly well-chosen?
3. Give instances of present participles used graphically and dynamically.
4. Characterize the dialogue in this story—what makes it especially realistic?
5. What new thing does the narrator discover about Jesus, and how does he respond to it?
6. Evaluate the statements of each parent about Jesus.
7. Why does the boy start getting dressed to go outside in the cold?
8. How does the sled relate to what the boy has just learned about Jesus?

MILDRED ZYLSTRA

Pink Peppermints

Martha frowned as she tapped lightly on Gran's door. This room should be hers. It would be if Gran had some other place to live. Mother said it was nice for sisters to room together, but it wasn't, especially now that she went to Junior High and could stay up later than Mary Alice. She hoped Gran would not hear her soft knock, but as she turned to go she heard the familiar "Come in."

She entered so quickly Gran had no time to take her feet down from the radiator. But Gran didn't seem to mind. She pushed her glasses up on her forehead, and smoothed her apron. Why did Gran have to wear aprons? Black ones in the morning, white ones in the afternoon.

Gran dropped the newspaper on the floor and edged herself carefully out of the big plush rocker. "I didn't know it was so late," she said as she shuffled across the carpet. "My clock stopped again, the *Gekke Betje.*"

Foolish Betsy—that's what Gran called her clock. Why didn't she have it fixed, Martha wondered again. The gold trimming on the black enamel case was chipped and Gran had propped up one broken leg with a little blue pillbox.

"Four more inches, I see by the paper, and the river will be over the banks," Gran said.

"Father says there's no danger."

"That's how Noah's friends talked. Water and women, your Granfather used to say, nobody knows what they'll do."

"We don't have to worry. The water can't reach us here."

"For shame to talk so. What about the poor folk down by the

river? Back in the Old Country when the dyke broke. . . ."

"I know, Gran," Martha interrupted. "You've told me the story. Mother says I should go right to bed."

"So you should. Your sister was here long ago." Gran jerked at the gilt knobs of the dresser.

Martha wrinkled her nose as she smelled the mothballs. Everything in the room was old and ugly, she thought, as she looked at the sagging featherbed and the bulging yellow plush rocker.

"Here, girl," said Gran, holding out two pink peppermints.

"Thank you." At the touch of Gran's cold fingers Martha shivered a little. She didn't want to touch Gran's ring. There was a groove all around it filled with a tiny braid of hair. The hair belonged to Lisbet and Anneke, Gran's little girls who had died. Martha pulled her hand away and walked to the door, murmuring, "Goodnight."

"Och now, where did I lay my specs? Did you see them girl?"

"They're right on your head."

"So they are!" Gran pulled the glasses down on her nose. "That's the second time today you've found them. Tomorrow I'll give you a nickel for your bank."

"Could I spend it instead?"

"For what? I give you candy. You save the money."

Martha stepped into the hall and closed the door. The nightlight left a deep hedge of shadow along the wall. Martha hurried into her own room, the room that was only half hers. She saw that Mary Alice was almost ready for bed. That meant she would have to hurry and turn off the light.

"I'm sick of going in to see Gran every night," she said, slamming the door. "She wants to tell the same old stories."

"I like them," said Mary Alice, pulling on her pajamas. "Remember how we used to listen to them after Mother thought we were in bed?"

"It was fun when she first came to live with us," said Martha. "But all her stories are stale now. I'm not going in every night any more."

"You don't have to stay. She just likes to have us come in and say goodnight. I don't mind."

"That's because you're only eleven. Wait till you're in Junior High. You won't want to be treated like a baby then, either." Martha rattled the peppermints in her hand.

"Why don't you eat your candy?" Mary Alice folded back the bedspread.

"Do you know where Gran keeps it? In the drawer with her black stockings and her winter underwear. When I told her I didn't want any candy, she thought I was sick of horehound drops. That's why we get peppermints now. She gave me two tonight." Martha threw them on the dresser.

"I guess she gave you an extra one because she thought you were mad at her." Mary Alice took a running jump and leaped into bed.

"She promised me a nickel too."

"You're lucky."

"Lucky nothing. What good's a nickel if I have to put it in the bank?"

"You can get interest on it, Gran says. Why were you so cross with her at dinner tonight?"

Martha licked her sticky hand. "Why did Gran have to tell Mother about our room? She knew we didn't have time to make the bed this morning." Martha pulled her hair back from her forehead as tightly as Gran wore hers. Shuffling across the carpet without raising her feet, she muttered, "Och toch! Those girls! Such a nest!"

Mary Alice giggled. "Why do you suppose she calls it a nest? I don't see why you're mad. Gran made the bed for us. She just wanted Mother to know she had done something. She didn't tell to be mean."

"Maybe not. But I don't tell Mother on her. I know something too."

"What?" Mary Alice sat up quickly.

"I don't think I should tell you."

"Please!"

"You're too young to know."

"Please," begged Mary Alice. "I'll make the bed alone in the morning if you'll tell me."

Martha tiptoed to the bed, and whispered, "I've guessed it for a long time. Yesterday I found out for sure."

"What?"

"She chews tobacco!"

"Are you sure? How do you know?"

"Never mind how I know. I just discovered it." Martha nodded solemnly as Mary Alice stared at her. "You mustn't tell Mother. She wouldn't want us to know."

"I never tell things." Mary Alice gulped as her peppermint slid down her throat. "I don't think it's so awful anyway," she added.

"Well, I do. And I'm sick of the way Gran eats. She slobbers."

"That's because she's losing her teeth."

"Then why doesn't she get store ones?" Martha brushed her hair with long hard strokes. "Rose is coming to dinner tomorrow night. I wish Gran didn't have to eat with us."

"Rose won't mind."

"Is that so! You wouldn't say that if Rose were your friend. You're just too young to understand." Martha swung the hairbrush. "I'm not the only one in this family who's ashamed of Gran. I heard Mother tell Father that she hated to have anyone go upstairs and see the awful old furniture in Gran's room. But Gran won't let her change a thing; she says it's the only thing she asked when she came here to live — to have her own furniture in her room. Mother says people will think she doesn't want to spend money for Gran, but Gran won't even let her buy her a new chair."

"Mother's not ashamed of Gran. She says she's got spunk. She says she knows more than is written in books."

"She does funny things, though. Like carrying her money in her underskirt! She lifts up her dress and takes out her money right in the store. You know she does!"

"She stands up close to the counter."

"But everybody sees her. What will people say?"

"Just that she's an old lady." Mary Alice leaned back on her pillow.

"Old lady indeed! That's no excuse. Are you going to carry money in a pocket in your underskirt when you're old? And eat *soepen brei?*"

"I don't like buttermilk."

"Of course not. Nobody does but Gran. It smells sour. I don't see why she can't eat it in her own room. Do you suppose—" Martha stared at her reflection in the mirror—"do you suppose she would eat in her own room—just for tomorrow night? I'm going to ask her."

"What would you say?"

"I'll tell her I'm going to bring her dinner upstairs for a change, like in a hotel."

"You can't fool Gran. She'd be hurt. Mother says she hates to feel she is in the way."

"You just stick up for Gran because you're her favorite. She thinks you're named for her. How would you like to be called Alt-je? Mary Altje—that's a nice name, isn't it?"

"I'm named after Mother."

"Oh no, you're not. Father calls her Mary, but Gran named her Martje. That's where I get my name."

"Well, anyway, Mother won't let you talk to Gran."

"I won't ask her. I'm going right in Gran's room now."

"Don't go," said Mary Alice. "You mustn't!"

"I'd like to know why not!"

"It isn't nice."

"Little goody-goody!"

"I'm not. But it'll make Gran feel bad. Please don't, Martha."

"You needn't preach to me. I said I was going and I am." Martha threw down the hair brush and opened the door.

She walked slowly down the dark hall. She would get Gran to tell her a story, and then ask her about the dinner. Mary Alice was right: Gran would be hurt. Besides, Mother wouldn't stand for it. If only Gran were in bed! Then she wouldn't have to ask. Martha tiptoed to the door. Her heart sank as she saw the light through the keyhole. If she went back, Mary Alice would think she was a fraidy-cat. She held one foot against her leg to warm it.

Suddenly she stiffened into attention. Gran was talking aloud. Her voice came in a muffled monotone through the door. What could she be doing? Cautiously Martha turned the knob, pressed against the panels, and put her face to the opening.

Gran was kneeling beside the bed in a long-sleeved flannel nightgown. Her hair hung down her back in a thin little braid.

Martha swallowed a laugh and pressed close to the door. Gran was talking Dutch. Martha heard her name, then Mary Alice's. Gran was praying for them. Martha held her breath to listen. Johannes — that was Grandfather. She caught another word — the Comforter. The minister had preached about that on Sunday, and said that He came to the apostles with the sound of a rushing wind and sat on their heads in little tongues of fire. Mary Alice wondered if the tongues of fire had burned the apostles' hair.

Martha gasped as the wind stirred the curtains at the open window. She pushed the door wider so that she could see if anything happened. Gran went on talking; then she stopped as if she were listening. Martha listened too, but there was no sound until Gran said, "Om Jesus' will, Amen." She looked thin and very small kneeling beside the bed. Her shoulder blades stuck out through the flannel, and Martha could see the veins, blue and bunchy, in her right leg.

Gran backed stiffly to her feet. With a start Martha remembered that she was eavesdropping. She pulled the door shut softly and tiptoed down the hall. She had never thought about Gran being lonesome before.

When she entered the bedroom, Mary Alice bounced up from the pillows. "You didn't ask her, did you?" she said.

Martha shut the door. "Well," she said, "I had a chance to see Gran's leg."

"The one with the very close veins?"

"Varicose, silly." Martha tossed her robe over the chair.

"Did you ask her?" insisted Mary Alice.

"She was busy talking."

"To who?" Mary Alice's eyes grew wide. Martha was always making discoveries.

"To God. She was telling Him all about us. I didn't want to interrupt."

"Don't ask her, Martha, and I'll give you those blue beads you always want to wear. I wish you would turn off the light. I'm sleepy."

"All right." Martha switched off the light and smiled. She would give the beads back. But now Mary Alice couldn't call her a fraidy-cat.

"I feel kind of sorry for Gran," said Mary Alice. "She misses Grandpa."

Martha thought how little and lonesome Gran looked kneeling beside the bed. "I guess we'll just have to put up with her," she said.

But as she undressed she felt angry again. She wanted to write in her Journal. If she were going to be a Great Author, she had to keep a Journal. All great writers did, her teachers said. She wanted a room of her own so she could write every night. Mother said she couldn't leave the light on long and keep Mary Alice awake; she didn't understand that Great Authors had to write about the things that happened each day.

She turned off the light, opened the closet door, switching on the hanging bulb, and closed the door. She pulled her Journal from a box of old clothes — Mary Alice had promised not to read it, but it was safer to keep it hidden. She sat on the floor, her back against the wall, and sucked on the pencil as she thought how lonely Gran looked talking about Grandpa Johannes.

Suddenly she got up, went into the bedroom and picked up the peppermints from the dresser. Mary Alice turned to watch.

"Remember how Gran's hat fell into the water when she crossed Deer Creek on the stepping-stones with us last week?" Martha said.

"That's because you let her hand go when you saw the frog," said Mary Alice.

"But I fished the hat out of the water for her," said Martha. "Didn't she look funny when she put it right back on her head?"

"She said it would shrink if it dried on the grass," said Mary Alice. "I don't think she's funny; I think she's fun."

"Maybe we can get her to sing one of her songs for Rose," said Martha, "like *'Tikke takke toonen; 't Varkentje in de boonen.'*"*

She went back into the closet and closed the door. The floor was hard, and she pulled a sweater off a hook. "I'll be a starving artist in an attic," she thought as she picked up her Journal.

She put a peppermint in her mouth as she thought again about Gran. It sounded as if she were really talking to someone. She didn't just rattle off words as she and Mary Alice did when they prayed. She looked as if she were listening to someone.

Maybe Gran would tell her what God said to her.

After the first few sucks on the peppermint, the mothball taste went away. The candy taste came out—strong and spicy. It reminded her of Gran. She put the other peppermint in her mouth so Gran would not find it in the morning and think she was mad at her.

*a little pig in the beans

Questions for Discussion and Reflection:

1. What is the point of view in this story?
2. What is the central conflict in the story?
3. How does Mary Alice's attitude differ from Martha's? Why?
4. How does the author show the intimate union of the "natural" and "supernatural" in God's universe as Gran is kneeling in prayer?
5. What does Martha learn through the experience of eavesdropping on her grandmother?
6. Why does Martha eat the peppermints after all?
7. In the final paragraph, why does the mothball-then-candy taste of the peppermints remind Martha of Gran?
8. Why the names "Mary" and "Martha"?

LAWRENCE DORR

Lazarus

It was cold with the damp, bone-chilling cold of Florida winter days. They never lasted longer than two or three days at a time, but on days like those the sun would be dying, hidden behind a dirty white blanket. The wind was blowing, making the cedars whistle, rattling the leafless branches of trees and the remains of the corn.

The corn stood behind the house next to the vegetable garden, close enough for the waterhose to reach. It was a frame house with peeling white paint, rusting tin roof, and a front porch worn grey by the sun and rain. Looking along its side from front to back, one saw the house as the image of a Primitive Baptist Church; yet the front with its Neo-Gothic roof and Victorian stained glass suggested an Episcopal Church. Before being planted among the trees on a forty-acre farm, it had been an antique shop in town.

The house had been rented to a family of four. Some of the neighbors thought that the family had come from England, others that they came from South Carolina. But it didn't really matter since the closest neighbors lived a mile-and-a-half away and were not inclined to visit. They saw the children at the side of the road waiting for the school bus every school day and they glimpsed the wife driving to work. She was a small woman with auburn hair and a sweet face. The children must have taken after her. The husband was big. He had black hair, brown eyes, and wide cheekbones. He didn't go to work anywhere as far as anyone knew. He did a little dirt farming and bought the groceries. He had an accent, but nobody knew what kind since it wasn't Cuban.

Once when he was at the grocery store and was asked about his nationality he said: "I am an American," and scowled.

Now he was in the kitchen waiting for the water to boil so that he could make tea for his daughter Sibet, who was home with a sore throat. He shouldn't have been glad but he was. As a tiny girl she followed him around like a puppy dog and he loved her with a love that had overwhelmed him since he first saw her. The nurse had brought her out from behind a glass wall and he had asked to hold her. Holding her in his arms, looking at this perfection, he lifted her to thank God. The nurse took her away.

The kettle began to whistle. He made tea, enjoying the steam warming his face. The only heat in the house came from the kerosene stove in the alcove populated by two dogs, between the bathroom and the children's bedroom.

"Here is your tea, Sibet," he said.

"Thank you, Daddy." She was nine years old with a lovely nose, green-grey eyes, and dark-brown hair in pigtails. The room was painted sky blue, which made it seem filled with light. One window looked out on the desolation of the vegetable garden.

"How is your throat?"

"Much better."

"Shall we talk about our donkey cart or the four ponies who will pull our little stagecoach? . . . Twenty-five cents a ride."

"I think Johnny should be the driver and you and I will be the bandits who hold up the stage," she said. "Of course we just pretend holding it up."

"Of course."

They talked realistically about feed prices and the likely stagecoach passengers and the names of the ponies, who were all pinto. By 11:30 the stagecoach route was extended to cover all the schools in town, and the business provided income to build a seventy-five-foot schooner, the *Elisabeth*. It was painted the same blue as the room and had red sails like the Thames coal barges. After six weeks of uneventful crossing (*no, no*, the girl said, *we saw porpoises dancing*), they glimpsed the Devon coast and were guided in by the blinking light that stood on Jubilee to direct the fishermen of Beer.

"The light is at the bottom of Jubilee next to the men's room, Daddy."

"You are right. . . . Should we run the boat up on the shingle?" He was surprised that he was thinking seriously about the landing. The fishermen used to nose into shore, jump out, attach the cable, get the rollers under while the winch was slowly pulling up the boat. But would that be possible with a seventy-five-foot schooner?

"I can smell it," the girl said, happily hugging her knees. So could he. The odor of drying seaweed, nets, and lobster pots; the salty wind that with the changing of direction became a fish & chips concentrate; the pine smells and the kale too that came down from the surrounding fields.

"Where we picked mushrooms," the girl said.

The fields divided by hedges were a huge eiderdown with deep green dominating the pattern. Seagulls circled the church steeple crying a harsh, heart-breaking, homesick cry to be answered by a flock of sheep grazing by Castle Rocks. Their mouths were full of dry winter grass, yet they sounded as if it were cotton wool. Above all, or perhaps around it all, was a rhythmic panting like an engine waiting at a railway station, the sea rolling the shingle.

"You left out the two little lambs, Daddy."

"To tell it, it has to be winter." He looked out of the window. The walnut was a stark, grey Vishnu against a stark, grey sky. When the wind blew hard, the Spanish moss swung out almost horizontal like acrobats on a flying trapeze. "And we need snow." There was another problem. "And Johnny should be along too."

"This time he won't be with us when we meet the two little lambs because he is in school," the girl said. The man marveled how easy it was for the child to move back into the past and alter it so that the present would fit it. He saw the day too, but for him nothing had changed: snow on the ground and piled up on the hedges, Grandfather in his grey tweed shooting cape walking straight-backed, his curly white hair uncovered, followed by Freya the collie, John, Sibet, and himself bringing up the rear.

The gulls were swooping and diving, wisps of cloud against the church steeple. He remembered and felt the affection they had for each other and he thought that if needed he would die for them, knowing that the proof he used was absurd, yet it could not be helped. And testing, testing, he again stood before the wall facing the alien soldiers and their guns, letting the horror wash over him to make sure that if he must he could do it. Then without any preliminaries he was in the oddly shaped drawing room. The sun rays touching the curtains turned into pink splotches on the wall opposite. There were flowers in the marble fireplace. Grandfather sat next to them on a low chair.

"Where there is a spark of love there is a spark of spiritual life," he said. Outside the gulls were crying.

"Daddy," the girl said, "you still didn't tell it." And because the man was lost in thought, she told it herself. "Grandfather stays behind so that Freya should not scare the sheep and you and Sibet go down toward the flock of sheep and two little lambs come jumping and skipping toward the little girl. . . . Can you see it, Daddy?"

"You put your arms around them," he said, noticing that her face crumpled. "What's the matter?"

"My head hurts," she said, lying down. He brought two aspirins and a glass of water.

"This is pink children's aspirin."

The girl choked on the second aspirin but in the end got it down. "They were not cuddly, Daddy."

"Who?"

"They were not cuddly and they felt damp and oily and stuck together. The wool wasn't soft the way it looked." She began to cry.

"Why didn't you tell us if it mattered so much?"

"I didn't want Johnny to know. He was such a sweet little boy." She cried in earnest now.

"He still is, starting second grade." He touched her forehead. "You have fever and that is why you feel bad. I'll go outside with the dogs and let you sleep awhile."

As soon as the dogs heard "outside" and "dogs," their tails beat on the kerosene stove. He went to get his gun, thinking that as the world judged he was a failure because he couldn't get a paying job, and work itself was not honored, so that his farming counted for nothing, yet he was happy and felt whole. His wife, his children, his dogs loved him, the soil in their garden was rich, and there was always enough to eat.

Of course that did not account for the sense of his own value that allowed him the joy of others' success or to feel the pain of their tragedies. He reached the gun rack and the next instant there was an illumination. It could not be called anything else. What he saw was a box very much like the boxes he had seen in the National Gallery at Trafalgar Square, boxes fabricated by seventeenth-century Dutch artists, containing different rooms, some with their owners in them, all done in perfect scale. His own box was open at the back and he was looking toward the nave where four people were kneeling. He recognized himself, his wife and children. The dogs were there too, their ears softly relaxed, their forepaws piously crossed. Then he looked at the great light at the altar, a golden light, and his heart began to beat with the slow booming of bells just brought into motion. Instead of the chalice and the ciborium, he saw the Lord standing there surrounded by this curious light that made him finally under-stand the word *Glory,* and he longed with an infinitely sad longing to touch His feet. He reached out, feeling tears well up.

Outside it was bleak, the damp cold making him shiver. The dogs ran through the pecan grove. Gusts of wind tore at the Spanish moss; then he was through the grove and into an old field. It was there that the dogs struck, their voices high, excited, going toward the swamp, disappearing in it, then coming back. He saw them coming toward him but there was no rabbit in front of them. Not far from him they stopped, sheepishly looking from him to a clump of grass. He couldn't read the dogs at all. Then he saw them too and breaking the gun open pocketed the shells. The three little rabbits kept perfectly still. Looking at them close up was an affirmation of Durer's mastery. They were grey-brown-white in color. One had dark fur inside its ears. They looked soft.

A second later he scooped up the rabbits and put them into the front pocket of his sweatshirt, knowing that now the mother would never come back for them but not thinking of this. He thought of his daughter. The rabbits felt soft like butterflies palpitating on yellow flowers.

The man was driving back from town with the groceries and a bagful of slightly spoiled greens. The greens were for the rabbits, who had survived feedings with dolls' baby bottles and the dogs' sanitary lickings and were now ready to be turned loose.

The car turned off Highway 441 onto a side road, passed a log house with a TV aerial, a quonset hut seemingly filled with baying hounds, then Sunshine Stables, and turning left by a pond covered with duckweed, drove up to the house. Seeing it, the dog hanging over his shoulder began to lick his face. The other one lying on the back seat sat up ready to leave the car. They were home.

Up the front steps carrying the grocery bags, across the house into the kitchen—vegetables into the icebox, staples into the larder—then he was ready with a handful of lettuce. The rabbits lived in a basket in the alcove. They were not in their basket but that was all right; jumping out of the basket was a sign of progress. He found two of them under his son's bed and put them back into the basket. Their noses wrinkled as they nibbled the lettuce.

After awhile the man stopped watching and decided to get the third rabbit, the one with the dark fur inside its ears.

By the time he searched the bathroom, feeling the cracked linoleum against his face as he peered under the tub, it ceased to be a routine getting the rabbits back into the basket. The rabbit with the black ears was definitely lost.

He went outside to get help from the dogs, but they had gone hunting on their own. Back again in the house he was assailed by nameless fears starting in his body that froze like a bird dog coming up on a covey. He knew that this was ridiculous, thinking of the real horrors cataloged and presented in neat pablum jars for five minutes of every hour in the ceaseless litany of a fallen world. He was looking only for a lost rabbit. Then he noticed the back door of the kitchen ajar and there was new hope: the back porch was screened in and its door always closed.

The floorboard creaked under his feet. He looked down. The

rabbit was lying on its side stretched out, rigor mortis already set in.

"God," he said aloud. "God." The rabbit in his hands felt like a wet glove frozen dry. He thought of his children he wanted to shield but could not, remembering their faces when they were told that their only living grandfather was dead.

Tomorrow was Saturday, and the whole family would have taken the rabbits to Oleno State Park, where there was no hunting, and turned them loose. Just one more day. Seeing their joy that had never been—the rabbits disappearing in the woods, the children jumping up and down, and the two of them standing together, watching all this like reading poetry together—he moaned.

He should have gone outside to get a shovel, but instead he went inside to the alcove. The two rabbits were in their basket on a table next to the kerosene stove. There was a smaller basket on the table, and he put the dead rabbit in it. With God everything is possible, he thought, not believing it. He stood there, not feeling or thinking any more. Then he screamed. The dead rabbit had jumped at his chest. He was holding it in his hands now, away from himself, feeling a revulsion he had not felt with the dead body, and he put the dark-eared rabbit with the others. He knelt ponderously, his body almost bent to the floorboard as if heavy weights were pushing down on his shoulders. His lips said thank you, but he was thinking that he was an ordinary man who forgave himself too much for too many things, a man who hated injustice so much that in turn he was unjust himself. He had asked not expecting an answer, and he had been answered. He had seen his own Lazarus. It was unbearable.

On Saturday it was sunny and the river glinted as they walked over the suspension bridge. There were a lot of people at Oleno. Families cooking hot dogs and hamburgers, the smoke of their fires going up straight toward the sky. There were young people everywhere and even some Northern visitors braving the river. His children carried the basket on the bridge, but once they were over he asked them for it. He lifted the kitchen cloth, looking at the rabbits. They all seemed to have black fur inside their ears.

He couldn't tell them apart.

He walked to the edge of the woods and gently dumped them out of the basket. His children were jumping up and down. He was standing beside his wife, watching the rabbits disappear into the woods.

Questions for Reflection and Discussion:

1. Which words in the first paragraph are most important for developing the atmosphere? Find one other paragraph that uses setting for similar tonal effects.
2. Characterize the relationship of this father to his wife and children. Why does it differ from the relationships presented in most television dramas?
3. Which of our senses does Dorr engage in his narration? Point out several such descriptive passages.
4. In what way is Sibet's memory of the lambs a premonition?
5. How does the main character's "illumination" fit into the story?
6. What pattern do you see in the several references to color, paintings, and poetry?
7. Does the rabbit die? Does it really come alive again, or does the man only imagine that?
8. At the end of the story, why do *all three* rabbits seem to have black fur inside their ears?

EVERETT L. HUIZENGA

Without a Riderless Horse

He held the pen's cap, then eased it slowly over the tip which had linked mind and paper, considering again the insert added to the final page of the typed draft. Satisfied, the man snapped the parts of the executive's tool together, laid it aside and collected the mended pages, thumping them gently into alignment on the desk top. Finished. The last duty as secretary and general counsel of the company he knew he would one day head. Now the mile as executive vice president, nearing the last step, the last of many in the climb to which life had been given.

He removed glasses necessitated by that time of life when one's arms begin to shorten. His library was located at the far end of the west wing of the house. As he rubbed his eyes, the room's stillness brought him the awareness of being alone. This man didn't much like being alone anymore. He imagined now the memory of a liking of solitude, as a boy, on the farm.

He was tired. The smoke from the cigarette, again instinctively fired, hurt his eyes. It must be late. He studied his watch but the dial was unresponsive. He couldn't figure out if it read quarter after twelve or three o'clock. As he forced his mind to concentrate on the answer, the phone rang twice. The third ring startled him.

"Hello?" Who could be calling now; the watch was on speaking terms again. Two minutes after three. Silence. "Hello?"

"Is that you, Lieve?" His mother again. The Dutch term of

baby-like endearment grated as it touched his ear. She had already called him twice the evening before. She was always calling him these days. About nothing. At times forgetting and calling about something she had called about minutes before. An emotion, a feeling kindred to anger, welled through the man. This time she was crying.

There was no way the emotion could have been fully explained. Maybe she was too old, had lived too long. It was senseless — to be eighty and dying of cancer. Maybe she symbolized his own age, too young to be where he was, too old to turn back. Maybe she forced him to remember times long ago, times he didn't like to think about, for he imagined he was happier during those times.

Her baby. The latecomer. A good son, maybe the best of the lot. Except for Jake, couldn't be sure about him. How much can one judge from nineteen years? But as for himself, he was a good son. Who had bought a house and moved her from the farm, across country, when Dad died? Who supported her now? Who would get her in the best old people's home in the city if it came to that? Who visited her once a week, made his own children visit their Grandmother once a week? Who listened to the phone every day, always echoing something of no consequence, the cracked talk of age, of the past?

Maybe it was her pain, the almost unbearable pain. Even the little pills weren't doing their job, although they probably owned her now. He did suffer, helplessly, for her pain.

"Is that you, Lieve?"

"Yes, Ma. It's me. It's three in the morning, Ma. What's the matter?" She had called several times in the middle of the night lately.

"I had to talk to you—."

He interrupted. "Did the doctor send you new pills, Ma? I talked to him a couple of days ago. He said he would. I know how bad the pain is. Is that why you're calling?"

"I got the pills. They don't help much more than the others." Her voice thickened as she paused, searching for words to go on.

How many tears in eighty years, he thought. "That's not what I called about." Another pause. It seemed only one sentence could come out at a time. "I didn't know it was so late. Time don't matter much any more."

The emotion was only momentary; it now drained from him. As if in apology, as if to embrace her, he held the phone with both hands. "That's O.K., Ma. I wasn't in bed yet." When time had mattered, she wouldn't have liked his being up at such an hour. "Go on, Ma. What did you call about?"

"It won't be long now, Lieve." Voids spaced sentences. "I'm getting ready to answer the questions." Oh, what next, he thought. "There are going to be lots of questions, you know. And I got to be ready to answer them. I've been going over all of them. I didn't want to bother you. But I got to get something right with you."

"Oh, don't worry about anything like that, Ma." He was suddenly uncomfortable, wishing she wouldn't go on about Heaven's gate, wishing she would just ramble about nothing as usual. An odd wish, especially for a church-type son. More especially for a member of a type-church in which she and Dad had raised him. He couldn't think of anything to say next. How different he was from Dad. He said that to himself.

"I think I'm ready for most everything."

"I know you are, Ma."

"I can't help it about Ralph." He felt it coming, the review of her children, her precious contributions to the world. Maybe her only contributions. "Hannah either. They always went to church when they were home. Dad and me tried to tell them."

"I know, Ma."

"I think I told Hannah again when I wrote her. I think I wrote her. I can't remember if I wrote."

"I'm sure you did, Ma." He wished she would call him "Lieve" again.

Her voice broke. "I wish I knew where Ralph was. He moved. Did I tell you? His letters come back to me. Did I tell you he moved, Lieve?"

"Yes, Ma. You told me." Four years ago. That one had always been a bum. Grieved his folks, mistreated his wife, ignored his children. Everybody he touched. Disappeared. Ran off four years ago. "You told me, Ma."

"Maybe you could try to find him sometime. I don't know where any of the five little kids are either. You being a lawyer. A lawyer could do that."

She didn't know what a corporation lawyer could or couldn't do. She didn't even know now that those kids weren't little anymore. Maybe she did know something about brothers and their keepers. "Is that what you called about, Ma?"

"No, I think I got that straight now. I worry about it though. Besse and Bert go to church, you know. I think most of their kids do too. They don't write very often."

"Jake joined church before he went in the army, Ma. You remember that?"

"Dad thought so much of Jake. I think he would have stayed on the farm. It was on Okinawa wasn't it? Isn't that in Japan? We could never figure why he had to go so young. I guess that don't matter much now. He was a good boy."

"Yes. Yes he was, Ma." The man could hardly remember his older brother. Only vaguely the one furlough he had after basic, the uniform he wore.

"Lieve, Mae said something to me the other day."

"What, Ma?"

"She said you two never spanked your children. She said you didn't believe you should. There are other ways."

"What's the matter about that, Ma?" And then the old voice gave way completely, weeping, breath held, interrupted by forced bursts, somehow the sound of age reverted to the time following the womb.

"I'm sorry, Lieve." She couldn't continue. Another pause. What was she going to say? "I'm so sorry now, Lieve. But I couldn't do anything else."

"Sorry for what, Ma? You don't have anything to be sorry for." As he waited, he contemplated the lie. Everyone has something to be sorry for.

"Dad said I should be more patient. But you were so stubborn we didn't know what to do."

"About what, Ma?"

"I remember spanking you when you were a little boy. I didn't want to, but I didn't know what else to do." She broke again.

"Oh, Ma. Ma. That's nothing to worry about. I don't even remember that. There's nothing you'll have to answer for about me." No, he thought, there was another who would have to answer about him when the time came. If such a time came. Now an odd thought added to the odd wish.

"None of the others were that way. You were so stubborn. You wouldn't let us cut your hair. You always wanted to wear one thing. You wouldn't put on hardly anything we wanted you to. Even on Sundays."

"But I don't remember that, Ma. I don't even remember. You *should* have spanked me if I was that way. I don't remember, Ma. Honest. That's O.K., Ma. Please. Don't worry about that. It's nothing."

"Dad said I should have been more patient. He said it would pass. He didn't want to hit you. But I spanked you. I didn't know what to do. I got mad."

"Stop, Ma. I don't even remember. I'm sure I needed it. I often think to myself that those were the best years of my whole life. I wouldn't think that if it weren't true, would I? It's O.K., Ma." It was true. That's why he tried to avoid thinking about them.

"The other ladies at church made fun of me."

"What, Ma? Made fun of you?"

"They laughed at me cause your hair was so long. Because you wore that play army suit to church."

"I think I remember the play army suit, Ma. I think I always wanted to wear that because of Jake." And now, after so many years, he did remember the suit, remembered fighting to wear it. Even when he had outgrown it. Fighting with his parents, even fighting at school if anyone made fun of it. Where had those memories been buried?

"I didn't want them laughing at me. I spanked you to make you get your hair cut. I finally burned that little army suit. You were too big for it anyway. I even spanked you when you cried so about that. You were that way about everything. You were just so stubborn."

"Oh, Ma, don't worry about that. I don't remember anything

bad about any of that." A little playing with the truth could do no harm. He was, after all, a lawyer. Somehow, his own imagined importance minutes before seemed crushingly unimportant now.

"Don't you really, Lieve?"

"No, Ma. Nothing bad. Only good. Jesus won't even bother to ask you about that, Ma." The possibility of the reality that such a thing could happen made him shudder. "That's the least worry you should have."

"Are you sure, Lieve? I been worrying about that lately. You're such a good boy. I had to get it right with you."

"I'm sure, Ma. Oh. Ma, there's nothing I could be more sure about."

"You don't remember, Lieve? You sure it's O.K.?"

"Ma, it's O.K. I'm sure."

They talked then of the old days. And as the two of them rambled on, they seemed truly the good old days. She spoke of those days with a sharpness he thought had left her years ago. The old lady's voice wasn't having as much trouble with tears anymore. He was the one now having trouble with them. Because of memories about such things as cleaning fish he caught at the creek. About the time he spilled a whole can of fresh milk because he was showing off while pulling the cart to the milk house. About the time the neighbor's dog killed his two little pet ducks. About the cage he made for the racoon his brother Bert caught by a toenail in a fox trap. About the fall from the haymow while trying to catch a pigeon. About the cast all of the kids at school wrote on. About such and other great moments in history.

Her tears were leaving. She was easing off into forgetfulness again. She was achieving a sort of peace. "Night, Lieve."

His tears were coming. His mind was being pushed and crowded with thoughts a busy corporation executive shouldn't have to be bothered with. His sort of peace was leaving him. "Night, Ma."

With one motion he returned the phone to its cradle and swept his arm across the desk, sending the stacked papers flying, to float aimlessly around the room. Why was he so upset? It was the sweetest talk he ever remembered having with her. But he didn't want to think about it.

He walked to the phonograph, slamming the lever to drop a favorite record into position, almost begging Bach to cleanse his mind of thoughts that frightened him. As he turned up the volume control, waiting, he realized that for some time he had pre-positioned these disks for just such occasions. Why, he thought? The realization puzzled him so deeply that the nasal voice had gone through several lines of the song before he even noticed.

He turned sharply, his son had been using it again. The kid had his own record player. Something about a dope addict. It must be the record Jimmy had begged him to listen to. He had been too busy. "—a hole in Daddy's arm where all the money goes—and Jesus Christ died for nothing I suppose." Now a cabinet was pointing a finger at him. Even the accomplishments achieved at Brandenburg couldn't help now. He stilled the machine's talking.

The thought of his mother's careful preparations for a conversation with God tore at his mind. Somehow a prayer seemed in order. His church life often called for that. It was easy. Out loud. In public. For and about others. But now. Alone. A moment of truth. He couldn't do it. Something sacred had been long lost. Where and when?

She would die soon, he thought. Her obituary would be short. Came from Holland seventy-five years ago. Had children named so and so. One prominent son lives in the city. No dignitaries, no Lion of Judah would walk behind her when she left. She was not a famous person. Her funeral would be without a riderless horse.

Oh, God. Maybe she is a famous person. Maybe she contributed more to the world than he realized. Maybe Jesus Christ didn't die for nothing.

The fact that he wanted to pick up and rearrange the papers rather than pray gave him the greatest moment of suffering he had yet known.

The man sat on the floor, trying to decide which of the two actions would most endanger his future years.

Questions for Reflection and Discussion:

1. Characterize the protagonist, and explain how he has changed since his boyhood.
2. What is the point of view? (Note the introspection.)
3. Why does the son fear to consider his mother's concerns and questions?
4. Explain "If such a time came. Now an odd thought added to an odd wish."
5. Why doesn't the man want to hear about his being spanked as a boy?
6. Why does the son begin crying? Why does he become so upset?
7. What conflict (dilemma) is the lawyer-son struggling with at the end? Explain the concluding sentence of the story.

HISTORICAL REALISM

Stories of the past are frequently written in a romantic tradition of exaggerated sentimentality and Gothic grotesquery, of ludicrously involved love relationships and roller-coaster adventures. But the three stories that follow avoid substituting such unrealistic and inartistic conventions for an authentic presentation of the milieus and idioms of other ages. Plot, character, and theme remain basically the same.

Human nature has not changed since the Fall of Adam and Eve in Eden. Furthermore, the problems that man faces in God's world are compounded most of all by the wickedness of the human heart. Hawthorne was right about that; but his tragedy was his unwillingness to accept the Scriptural solution to that central human corruption: the Lamb of God who takes away the sin of the world. That is why the gloom of Hawthorne and Melville, for example, was so seldom relieved — except for occasional glimmerings of human fortitude and earthly wisdom, the gospel of stoicism and self-redemption.

"The Payment Is Blood" presents a ritual of atonement in the fatalistic tradition of Sophocles' *Oedipus* and Shakespeare's *Othello,* a purgation by self-sacrifice, in which suffering pays for sin. For if man will not accept the catharsis of Calvary, he becomes, by default, a victim of his guilt-ridden conscience and a plaything of deterministic forces. When the righteousness of Christ is repudiated, there remains only a certain fearful expectation of judgment and a desperate, fantastic attempt to be reconciled to cosmic justice, even if it be by suicide.

"Sign of a Promise" and "Through Devious Ways" are stories about the Dutch immigrants who settled in the Midwest. Their struggle with the land, the weather, with their dreams, their fears, selfishness, anger, and hatred — with the whole gamut of human tribulations and temptations, misery and sin — is rightfully subordinated in these narratives to the true calling of mankind: to discover the will of God and, then, by His Holy Spirit, to do it! That vocation, implicit in these stories, is the source of the profound peace and deep-flowing joy with which these works culminate. They reveal once again that the body of Jesus Christ (His people, His Church) becomes strong through weakness and through the keenly chastening love of our Father in Heaven.

E. WILLIAM OLDENBURG

The Payment Is Blood

For the Rev. Richard Whitehill the wilderness held no more terrors than the inner landscape of his Presbyterian conscience over which his doubts and conflicting motives portaged like *voyageurs* in search of the ultimate river passage to a land of peace and certitude. Whitehill had undertaken the actual journey from Mackinac Island down the long shore of Lake Michigan by canoe for two reasons. The official reason, which he had carefully stated in a letter to his home church in Massachusetts, was that his health required a vacation and change of scene if his continuing missionary work among the Indians at the fort was to be effective. The other reason, which he scarcely admitted to himself, was the lure of the fur trade and the vague unspoken promises of challenge and opportunity which the wilderness held out.

Whitehill had taken his missionary post on the island in 1815, shortly after the end of the War of 1812. He had left New England with no regrets, exchanging the settled decorum of Massachusetts for the unknowns of the frontier. He had been surprised during the first year of his stay to discover in himself a facility for learning the Indian languages which his struggles with Greek and Hebrew in seminary had scarcely led him to expect. Despite the success of his linguistic adventure, however, Whitehill soon found life on Mackinac lacking the variety and excitement he had hoped for. The small band of Indians who worshipped at his Protestant chapel each Sunday remained as static and unchanged as the most staid congregation in Amherst. His mastery of Ojibway and Ottawa, Whitehill felt, gave him no clue to the real lives of these people, nor did the rudimentary theology he taught them seem to touch them in any essential way. They seemed, these "savages" of his, to be oddly tamed and subdued in the looming shadow of Fort Mackinac. They lisped the creeds with the happy simplicity of children, and Whitehill grew restive with it all. The green wooded beauty of Mackinac Island itself, surrounded by the breathtaking blue of the straits, seemed to Whitehill a child's fairy paradise, insulated, isolated from the real world. He might as well, he thought, go down to the pebbly shore and skip flat stones across the blue water as prepare and preach his childish sermons week after week.

But the real world intruded into the island paradise. With the end of the war the fur trade burgeoned, and while Whitehill's congregation remained static, the following of the fur traders multiplied. The seekers of pelts outbid the savers of souls, and instead of homilies and hymns they brought cloth and guns and whisky. Officially Whitehill inveighed against their practices; secretly he viewed their invasion each spring as the raucous breath of reality blown in over the cold waters of the straits. They brought their pelts in from remote trading posts around the lakes, from Green Bay, from the mouth of the Muskegon, the Grand, the St. Joseph, from Chicago.

In Chicago, at the southern-most point in their journey, Whitehill had written in his journal: "April 20, 1819; Our stay in Chicago is almost at an end, for Deschamps has informed me that tomorrow or the next day we must embark again and turn our canoes north. Our first camp will be made at the Grand Calumet and from thence to the mouth of the St. Joseph. Deschamps hopes to reach the mouth of the Grand at the time of the May full moon, for it is then that the Indians gather to fast and feast their dead. Our stay here has been a welcome respite from the rigors of the long journey down the lake. We have cabins to sleep in here, albeit somewhat rude ones—a welcome change nonetheless from the tents that were our nightly abodes enroute. Young Gurdon Hubbard was just in to see me to ask how I was feeling. He is a considerate and most civilized young man. I pray that Deschamps and the older, rougher traders will not corrupt him. He and Deschamps were surely right about one thing: the trip has so far done wonders for my health. My cough has well nigh disappeared, and the exercise and fresh air have strengthened me more than I would have imagined possible. At first I was able to do very little paddling, but as the days went by I was able to take a greater share in this strenuous activity until now I fear I am almost sinfully proud of my dexterity."

They loaded the canoes early on the morning of April 22nd. Deschamps was in a jovial mood despite his disappointment at the number and quality of pelts he had been able to acquire at the Chicago post.

"The Reverend will want to stay in the preaching business now that he sees what a poor thing the fur business is becoming," the fur trader observed to the minister. His laugh boomed across the water of the Chicago River.

"I think Monsieur Deschamps will not return to Mackinac penniless or peltless," Whitehill returned. The New England Presbyterian's relationship with the French Canadian Catholic was an easy and comfortable one. Whitehill, in fact, somewhat prided himself on his toleration of Deschamps' occasional irreverences.

"We will do much better at the mouth of the Grand," young Hubbard said. "The Indians will be gathered there for the Feast of the Dead."

"The Reverend can preach many funeral sermons there," Deschamps said, laughing again.

"I want very much to see these rituals," Whitehill replied immediately, his tone serious now. "I have learned all too little about the real beliefs and religious practices of these people from my contacts with them on the island. They treat me like a child. They tell me only what they think is safe for me to know."

Deschamps himself became more serious now. He had himself been educated for the priesthood, had rejected the calling of the cloth for marriage and the worldly business of fur trading, but still possessed, Whitehill felt, a profound devoutness as a Roman Catholic, and, despite his flippancies, a profound sense of the presence and endurance of the Holy Catholic Church, a genuine other-worldliness which led him to view all material goods as ultimately of no more value than the baubles he traded to the Indians. "We share one creed, you and I," he told Whitehill earnestly, "and it speaks of the resurrection of the body and the life everlasting."

"Yes," Whitehill said. "A victory over death."

"The Indian cannot think of such a thing," Deschamps said. "The Indian can think of victories over his human enemies, even over the white man, but he cannot think of victories over nature. And a victory over death would be like a victory over a flooded river, over a January blizzard, over a November gale on the lake. The Indian does not hope for such victories. He accepts such forces, avoids them when he can, tries to survive them. Death he can avoid for a time. He cannot survive it. He accepts it."

"The Feast of the Dead is a feast of mourning then?" Whitehill asked. "Not a feast of celebration?"

"I've seen more mourning than celebration at Christian funerals, for all your talk of victory over death," Robert Stewart said suddenly, breaking what had been for him a longer than usual silence.

Whitehill glanced at Stewart, considered several retorts, then decided to say nothing. Stewart's remark did not surprise him. He had carried on a running philosophical and theological battle with Stewart ever since coming to Mackinac where Stewart was one of the managers of the American Fur Company, second in authority only to old Ramsey Crooks. "Battle" was the only word for it, Whitehill reflected; no word so mild as "debate" would do. Stewart was a pugnacious Scotsman whose outrageously quick temper was a legend throughout the lake country. Early in Whitehill's stay on the island Stewart had nearly clubbed a man to death when he caught him stealing whisky. Stewart was a renegade Presbyterian, a child of the Enlightenment, an avid reader of Thomas Paine, whose ideas he flourished like a club in every argument.

Nonetheless, for reasons he never fully understood, Whitehill had liked the man from the start; he relished their ideological battles—"You are living in the past," he would tell Stewart; "your ideas belong to the last century; Deism and the worship of

Reason were only passing fads; they are as dead now as you mistakenly think Christianity is" — and he was usually able to hold his own, matching Stewart's arguments in cogency and logic if not in ferocity. But Whitehill was not in the mood now to take up Stewart's challenge. As their boats cleared the mouth of the Chicago River and slid north parallel to the heavily wooded shore, the minister felt, confronted by an infinity of lake and impenetrability of forest, an impatience with words and concepts as he had known and used them all his life. In the silence of lake and shore he listened for meanings.

In his tent at the mouth of the St. Joseph River, Whitehill wrote in his journal: "April 29, 1819: We have made what young Hubbard calls "a leisurely trip" from Chicago and are camped now very near a large band of Potawatomi, from whom, unfortunately, Deschamps was able to acquire very few additional pelts, the Indians having traded most of what they had to a rival fur company earlier in the spring. The Potawatomi, however, have assured us that there will be large numbers of Indians gathering at the mouth of the Grand for the Feast of the Dead, and Deschamps hopes for greater success there. We leave for that location very soon. In two or three weeks we will be back at the island, a prospect which creates conflicting emotions in me. I miss Anne and the two boys very much, but I have felt a freedom and exhilaration on this wide expanse of water which I have never felt in the confinement of my study, nor in the green insulation of Mackinac, nor in the bonds of family life and responsibility, sacred and precious as I must hold those bonds to be."

On the night before they were to leave the St. Joseph for the Grand, young Gurdon Hubbard visited Whitehill in his tent. Hubbard was only seventeen, had been only sixteen when he joined the American Fur Company as a clerk in the spring of 1818. He had spent the summer of 1818 on Mackinac, where Whitehill had met him and had liked him immensely from the start. Hubbard had spent the winter at Beebeau's trading post west of Chicago on the Fox River, keeping the records for the old illiterate trader who was by now virtually bed-ridden — ministered to all winter by an old squaw. As a result, young Hubbard, at seventeen, had run, in effect, the trading post.

Whitehill was not surprised that the company thought highly of the young man.

"Are you glad now that you came on this little trip?" Hubbard asked. "You must not mind some of the things Mr. Stewart says. He has a good heart and I'm sure he doesn't mean all of the terrible things he says."

Whitehill laughed. "Not *all* of them? Only some of them you mean?" Then he saw by the hurt look on the young man's earnest face that he had said the wrong thing. Hubbard was a serious young Christian, and Whitehill's laughter did not seem to him a proper response to the tragedy of Stewart's agnosticism and apostasy.

"I have known Robert Stewart for four years," Whitehill told him. "You are right when you say he has a good heart. He was the one, you know, who convinced me to come on this trip. He was concerned about my health. It is not with his heart, you see, that he rejects the faith, but with his mind. He prides himself in his reason, and so it is on the battlefield of reason that I must meet him. We must be all things to all men, as the apostle said, if we would hope to win some. You must not be alarmed if we sometimes appear to debate frivolously about the most serious matters, even joke about them. That is simply the way Stewart's mind works, and we are not being frivolous at all but deadly serious. Just pray with me that God may use my debater's skill and even my jests to turn one man's stubborn mind around. Then he may be as great a man in our Lord's kingdom as he is now in Mr. Astor's fur kingdom."

Young Hubbard looked thoughtful, if not fully convinced. "I pray that may happen some day," he said. He seemed reluctant to leave.

"How did you come by that scar on your forehead?" the minister asked, grateful for a chance to change the subject and noticing in the candle light a long well-healed scar as the young man brushed the thick hair back from his forehead.

"An Indian tried to tomahawk me last winter," Hubbard said, "because I knew he was unreliable and had refused to advance him supplies. He slipped up behind me while I was working on the account books and would have killed me if I had not seen his shadow on the wall. I turned just in time to block the handle of his weapon with my forearm, but the blade still struck me lightly here." He touched the scar. "He tried to draw a knife then, but I wrapped both of my arms around him and pinned his arms; we rolled on the floor until his struggle to free himself had exhausted him; then I picked up a stool and struck him with it."

The young clerk paused but Whitehill said nothing, sensing that the story was not finished. Still, Hubbard seemed reluctant to continue.

"The first blow knocked him unconscious," he began at last.

"And you could then call for help," the minister said.

"I could have," Hubbard said. "But I struck him again. Three or four times. As hard as I could." He paused again, and again Whitehill said nothing. "I wanted to kill him," he added finally.

The minister considered for a moment before he answered. "Such a rage would be very natural," he said. "After all, he tried to kill *you.*"

"Are we supposed to do what is natural?" Gurdon Hubbard asked. "Are we not supposed to love our enemies, to turn the other cheek?"

"Yes, of course, those were Christ's commands," Whitehill admitted. "However, there are times when—" He broke off, staring distractedly at the candle flame.

"There is more to the story," the younger man said. "I might as well finish it." He stared at the candle flame himself for a moment before going on. "The man I struck recovered, but very slowly. He was not able to do any more hunting or trapping all winter. Eventually some of the other Indians, ones who had been friendly toward me from the beginning and had taken my side of the issue, saying that I had a right to defend myself, came to me and begged me to make some restitution to the injured Indian. His injuries, they said, had taken away his means of livelihood."

"Did you make restitution?"

"I wanted to. I knew—and I'm not sure anyone else knew this—that the first blow with the stool would have been sufficient to disarm him, that his most serious injuries undoubtedly came from the three or four additional blows I had struck him. However, at the time, I was in sole charge of the trading post, Mr.

Beebeau being so ill as to be completely incapacitated. Therefore, whatever I did I would be doing for the company, and I would not be acting as a responsible agent of the company if I made restitution with company goods to an Indian who had tried to kill a company agent. It would set a dangerous precedent. So whatever I might feel I owed the person, had I been responsible only to my own conscience, I could pay him nothing as a responsible agent of the company."

Whitehill contemplated the young man's story in silence, and young Hubbard himself, apparently expecting no answer, said good-night and quietly left the tent.

The passage from the mouth of the St. Joseph to the mouth of the Grand was made rapidly and without incident. Lake Michigan was calm and the sun beat down with an intensity unusual for the early days of May so that the sand dunes of the shorelines seemed to waver and melt before their eyes.

"Does the parson look unto the hills from whence cometh his help?" Robert Stewart asked as Whitehill scanned the high wooded bluffs north of the mouth of the Kalamazoo. Whitehill had answered Stewart's last question about the immortality of the soul only with silence.

"The devil can also quote Scripture," the minister said with the smallest of smiles. Young Hubbard's moral dilemma was still on his mind, and he could not sustain his usual relish for philosophical debate with Stewart.

When the mouth of the Grand came into view, the voyageurs and halfbreeds manning the canoes and batteaux sent up a cheer; then the small fleet glided safely between huge sheltering dunes into the harbor mouth. Whitehill was particularly impressed by the size of the dune to the north of the river.

"A veritable Mt. Arrarat," Stewart suggested, noticing the minister's interest.

At the base of the dune, between it and the river, they could see wigwams and campfires. Strung along the south bank and on the island dividing the north branch from the south branch of the river were more Indian camps. The boats of the fur traders forged steadily upriver, taking the south branch; they passed a large clearing where, Deschamps said, the Indian women grew corn in the summer; they made camp just beyond the clearing in a grove of ancient beech trees.

That night Whitehill wrote in his journal: "May 4, 1819: Young Gurdon Hubbard was just in to talk again and had another rather strange Indian story to tell, the sequel to which, he says, we may be able to see for ourselves tomorrow. He has learned since our landing that the Indians camped here are in a peculiar state of excitement about a fugitive from justice (Indian justice, I take it) who is due to present himself at this site to face the punishment for his crime. The punishment, according to Hubbard, will certainly be death; for this man, the fugitive, killed the son of a chief last autumn in a drunken brawl and then disappeared. The Indians told Hubbard that they now knew he spent the winter at the headwaters of the Muskegon River hunting and trapping, hoping to amass enough pelts to ransom his life — such a transaction apparently being common in Indian custom and law. However, he has been unsuccessful and is now coming to answer in person for his crime. A scout has seen him, Hubbard was told, and the murderer is expected to reach the mouth of the Grand very soon, in all likelihood early tomorrow morning. Deschamps and Stewart and Hubbard and I will take one of the light canoes downriver to the Indian camps by the first light of morning in hopes of viewing this unusual spectacle."

The early light of morning broke through the high fringe of trees which formed the eastern boundary of a grassy hollow in the dunes south of the river's mouth and close to the shore of Lake Michigan. The four white men had beached their canoe on the shore of the lake where a light surf was rolling and had climbed the highest of the dunes enclosing the hollow. From their vantage point at the dune's summit the view was magnificent: directly below them the hollow already half filled with quietly waiting Indians, and more of them filing in through a gap in the dunes at the northeast corner of the hollow; to the north and east, lifting their eyes, they could see the river winding into its last bend before meeting the lake; behind them, turning completely, the western horizon, the blue-green expanse of lake, the steady reiteration of surf. Around them, in the trees, the birds sang.

"It appears you were right," Deschamps said to young Hubbard. "The savages are gathering for some special reason."

"I would lay two to one odds the man never appears," Stewart snorted. "More likely he's already somewhere west of the Mississippi. What sane man, even a redskin, would put his neck in a noose after he's already escaped once?"

"From what I've been told," Hubbard said seriously, "he never thought of himself as escaping, only as buying time to ransom his life, and he fully intended to return if he could not get enough pelts for the ransom."

Whitehill was silent. He had often enough in the past felt like a mere spectator at life's drama, but on this sunny May morning of light breezes and bird songs his feeling of spectatorhood was intensified and oddly altered. This hollow in the dunes may as well have been an ancient amphitheater, and the minister felt himself swept back in time to the world's first morning, felt as if primordial significances lay in wait for him, as if a ritual of revelation of which he may have dreamed eons ago were promising to unfold itself. The Indians had finished filing into the hollow. They stood silent, motionless, expectant. The opening which led aisle-like into the hollow was empty.

Whitehill and his companions became aware gradually of a sound which at first was scarcely distinguishable from the steady low sound of the surf behind them: rhythmic, insistent, repetitious. As the sound became louder, they realized that it was coming from the opposite direction. And then they identified the sound itself: a single drum, struck slowly, insistently, monotonously. The drumbeats, as they became louder, now quite clearly seemed to come from the same aisle by which the other Indians had entered the hollow. The drummer himself was still invisible, hidden in the shadows of the leaf arch, but even before the man came into view, the observers on the summit of the dune could hear another sound, a mournful chant for which the monotonous drum beat was only the accompaniment.

"He is chanting his own death song," Gurdon Hubbard whispered. The chant and the drumbeat became louder and louder until it seemed to Whitehill to fill the hollow entirely. He could no longer hear the birds singing.

An almost imperceptible movement among the Indians in the hollow—as if the breeze that Whitehill could feel in his hair had swayed them all slightly—signaled the apperance of the doomed man. He stepped suddenly into a broad band of sunlight that lay along the grassy aisle where it entered the hollow. He moved slowly, deliberately, head bent, drum tucked under left arm, right arm moving rhythmically across his body; he had thrown off his winter blankets and buckskins and wore only a small loincloth. His naked marching body looked emaciated, the legs so thin it was hard to believe they had carried him from the headwaters of the Muskegon River, his ribs visible even from the height of the dune where Whitehill and his companions sat; his bronze skin stretched tight over his bones, he was a covered frame, a draped skeleton marching toward death.

"Behind him," Hubbard whispered. "Look behind him. He has not come alone."

Walking behind the Indian, in single file, were a woman and three children. The woman wore a blanket, and one corner of it was draped over her head, hiding half her face; the children, all apparently under the age of ten, were clothed like their father—naked except for loin cloths.

"His family?" Whitehill asked Hubbard, discovering when he began to speak that his throat muscles were tight. "They look as emaciated as he does."

"They all nearly starved during the winter," Hubbard answered.

The drumbeats stopped, but the birds still sang. The Indian set his drum on the ground; his movements were slow, deliberate, ceremonious. With equal ceremony he motioned for his wife and children to seat themselves at his feet, while he straightened himself to his full height and stood as if at attention awaiting the approach of another Indian who had left the larger group and was advancing slowly to meet the fugitive. When they stood face to face, the fugitive began to speak. To the listeners and watchers atop the dune his voice sounded surprisingly strong and deep.

"He is speaking to the chief," Hubbard whispered to Whitehill. The minister nodded; he knew enough of the Ottawa language to follow most of what the fugitive was saying:

"In a drunken moment I stabbed your son. . . . I fled to the marshes at the head of the Muskegon, hoping that the Great Spirit would favor me in the hunt. I was not successful. Here is the knife with which I killed your son; by it I wish to die. Save my wife and children. I am done."

The chief accepted the knife solemnly, then turned and beckoned to someone in the crowd behind him. A young man separated himself from the group and came toward him.

"The chief's oldest son," Deschamps said. "Brother of the murdered one. I think I know what is to happen now. Better turn your head, preacher, unless you have a strong stomach."

The chief handed the knife to his son and gave a brief command. The young man, the knife clutched in his right hand, took two quick steps and stood face to face with the fugitive; he extended his left arm slowly, ceremoniously, as if making a salute or conferring a blessing; he placed his left hand on the fugitive's right shoulder and stood for a few moments motionless, as if waiting, it seemed to Whitehill, for a change of expression in the fugitive's face, a change which the chief's son did not really expect to see; waiting the obligatory moments nonetheless, not because tradition or ritual instructed him to wait, but because some instinct for decent order made him wait, made him mutely ask for a last futile plea, made him give the doomed man his chance to cringe, to grovel, to beg. Then he raised the knife. He feinted twice, three times, toward the fugitive's breast; there was no flinching, no change of expression; nor did the feints seem to Whitehill intended to produce any such reaction; they seemed more like preparatory, warm-up movements—like the circles penmanship pupils made in the air over their desks before committing their pens to paper. The fourth thrust was no feint. The knife-blade disappeared in the breast of the victim and was immediately withdrawn again.

For a few seconds, while bird song was the only sound, it seemed to the watchers on the dune that what they had seen must have been a stage trick done with a knife whose blade disappeared into the handle upon impact. For there was no change in the picture below. The victim had scarcely moved when the knife struck, and his expression was unchanged. But the illusion lasted for only a few seconds. The wound began to gush blood; a bright fountain splashed on the sand at the executioner's feet. In the numbness of Whitehill's mind the words of the hymn insinuated themselves: "There is a fountain filled with blood, drawn from Immanueal's veins. . . ." Beside him, young Hubbard had turned his head; he looked ill.

The stricken, still-standing man's body began to tremble; he crumpled suddenly but still noiselessly to the sand. The birds sang on—their song the only blemish on the morning's silence.

Questions for Reflection and Discussion:

1. How does the diction (word choice) of Whitehill's April 20, 1819 journal entry fit that historical period?
2. As Deschamps puts it, what unites the Roman Catholic and Protestant faiths in contrast to the Indian religion?
3. What is "Deism and the worship of Reason"?
4. Evaluate Whitehill's method of Christian witness to Robert Stewart, as Whitehill defends his approach to Gurdon Hubbard.
5. Do you accept Hubbard's explanation for not making restitution to the Indian whom he injured? That is, is it a Scripturally justified argument?
6. Does the device of the journal impede or advance the plot?
7. What are noteworthy details of setting in the execution scene?
8. How does the Indian's death compare to and contrast with that of Jesus Christ?

JAMES SCHAAP

Sign of a Promise

The longer he prayed, the deeper his knees sank in the moat of muddy topsoil that circled the sod house. The rain dropped from the gray sky like shot from a small-bore rifle, undeflected by the usual prairie winds. It punched little craters in the mud of the path, craters that vanished when others exploded in the soggy earth. He had removed his wide-brimmed hat and was holding it tightly to his chest with his right hand as he bowed his head. Rain pounded into streaky hair that lay like flax on his head, then streamed down through weathered crevices in his temples and forehead, dripping, finally, from the tip of his nose and chin onto his heavy overcoat, already saturated from three full days of rain.

He looked upward and turned to the west again to reassure himself of what he had seen. A layer of clear blue sky belted the horizon, tinted by the fire of the late afternoon sun, now dropping slowly from the cloud banks that still dominated the sky. Rain pelted his face, but he stared defiantly upward, the water running from the ends of his moustache, through the recesses of his cheeks, and into his scraggly gray sideburns.

To the east was the rainbow. It grew from two remote spots in the grassland, rising symmetrically toward a peak that was yet to appear. Its thick backdrop of rain clouds, suddenly curtained in purple by the sun, focused the colors, and made them burn almost mystically in the turbulent sky.

It wasn't the first time he had recalled Noah. Over a year ago he had left Wisconsin, taking his family in a "schooner," as the Americans called it, bound for Minnesota. Several months later, he and a few others left Fillmore County for northwest Iowa. Some of his friends seemed reluctant to give him their blessing. They watched silently as he loaded the wagon again, and they also saw his tired wife climb slowly up to take her place. There was some fear in the way they sang the psalms then, but Antonie Vander Meer remembered Noah and his neighbors — they had even mocked him, but Noah's faith was strong, and his mission even more of a test. Noah never questioned what the Lord had commanded him.

And then, the rainbow and the covenant. This was but three days, he told himself, three short days of rain. Noah had seen the heavens opened, the bowels of the earth erupt its inner waters, the entire world destroyed. Yet he had not questioned; he had not doubted. Antonie spat out the salty water that curled from his moustache into the corners of his mouth, rebuking himself for his little faith, while thanking the Lord for the fullness of His grace — a grace so rich it could even save one so wretched as himself. He bowed his head again and asked forgiveness.

A sudden downpour ladled more water over the land as the storm poured out the last of its offering. He raised his left hand to his forehead, brushed back the wet shock of hair that fell into his face, then replaced the hat on his head. He held his hands up to his face; they were pink and puffy, swollen from the water he had lived in for the last few days. But they were clean, except for the threads of black at the tip of each fingernail. And he was clean. Weeks of sweat and dirt had been washed away by the rain, transforming his spirit and body into readiness, into actual anticipation of what still remained to be done on the homestead. Now, as the end of the day approached and the almost-forgotten sun spread its warming rays out across the sea of prairie grass, lighting the eastern sky with God's own promise, now Antonie Vander Meer was ready for tomorrow.

He rose and walked carefully toward the sod pile that marked the corner of his land. As he left the immediate area of the sod house, however, the heavy grasses made the path more firm underfoot. To the left of the path lay a broad stretch of virgin soil, stripped of its mantle of flowers and grasses, already ravaged by the plow, and now left vulnerable to every whim of the Iowa weather—soil naked, rich, and fertile. He saw there what he had feared—the scars of the late spring storm, cracks and washes running like jagged bolts of lightning down the gentle slope, but emptied now of the rain water that they had carried during the long storm. His wife had walked every foot of that land, smoothing over the soil where the corn had been planted. Now the seeds were gone, he knew, washed from the earth as the chalky lines of gray had been washed from his temples, and carried by transient streams to some low spot on the land.

He didn't stop walking. He knew what he would find, but he needed to see the reality. Telling Tryntje would be difficult enough, so he knew he must be sure. When he arrived at the southern end of his field and saw the yellow seeds lying in clumps, he stopped, searching for words to explain it to her. He prayed for wisdom and strength. He leaned over, then, gathering the seeds into a pile with his clean hands. When he was through, he wiped his now-blackened palms against his trousers. He would return for the seed tomorrow. He stood and looked for a moment over the open prairie to the west and south, before turning back to the sod house. When he reached the path to the house, the rainbow had grown to a completed arch.

Tryntje, too, had seen the belt of clear sky on the horizon, but unlike her husband, she didn't focus on its promise. She concentrated once again on the wide wasteland that led to the sky, broad and barren, nearly unbroken by any sign of life. Occasionally, a cottonwood, white and lifeless, rose awkwardly from the prairie bed, interrupting the endless monotony of the landscape. One such monument stood at the southwest corner of their own land; it projected against a background of rainclouds now, its uppermost branches barely distinguishable. Tryntje saw it and thought of it as a pioneer too; for in its rash impulse to rise above the dour grassland, it had received jagged scars and gashes, which ran like stripes up and down its stubborn trunk. Finally, long ago, when no white man was yet foolish enough to settle here, one slashing blow of lightning had tamed its temerity forever. Now only a shell remained, a corpse that somehow refused burial, a frame that seemed to mock the vanity of its aborted dreams.

And the sky, spewing incessant rain, seemed to combine with the desert of grass to destroy whoever, whatever, tried to exist here. The endless expanse of prairie seemed to her a godless heath, and all the prayers she had learned as a child, no matter how loudly she would cry them to the heavens, could not bring her any closer to that God she had known in the old country. This land was so wide, so vast, so everlasting, that she felt her prayers rise in futility, like the fingers of that cottonwood, to a God who had never minded this region of creation.

But she never spoke these things to her husband. Through all those days that she saw her children blackened by the Iowa soil, roughened by the wind and sun, pushed prematurely into the experience of Adam's curse, and in all those hours she spent picking vermin from their young bodies, she had said nothing to him—for he was her husband. And she knew his visions, his dreams.

She turned from the window and looked back to the family portrait that hung on the mud wall. It had been taken in Wisconsin. She had wanted it immediately after their arrival in America to send to her parents in Holland, for she knew their concern and felt that they would be reassured by the clean faces and the Sunday clothes of the children. They knew very little of America. Some of the stories they had heard were like those of the land of Canaan—a land most bountiful, full of opportunity for all. But others were fearful accounts of drought, storms, savages, violence, strange and horrid stories of people who didn't know the Lord.

The family picture had helped, she knew, for it showed them tidy and happy, wearing the smiles that reflected the hopes and jubilation of a life filled with new opportunities. She knew they would like it, for she liked it. This was the way she imagined things. There were four pretty children on the tintype; now there were only three. But soon there would be another, unless her signs were false. She ripped the very thought from her mind—this was no place . . . no time for a child!

The bolt rattled and the uneven door swung open slowly.

"Tryntje?" It was her husband. He was wet and cold, but his face widened into a comforting smile.

"Tryntje? Did you see it? The sky, it is clearing! The rain will stop."

He set his hat on a nail that stuck from the wooden door frame, dropped his coat over another, and drew a wooden box away from the shipping crate they used as a table. He sat down and folded his hands before him, rocking comfortably back and forth, adjusting himself to the chair, still wearing the smile.

"That is good, Toon. I did see it. The rain will stop now. Tomorrow a bright morning . . ."

"Ja, Tryntje, tomorrow we will begin again."

She smiled at him momentarily, then poured him a cup of coffee.

"We have not much coffee left, Toon. You must appreciate this."

"We run out already?"

"Ja, not long."

"Ach, do we drink so much?"

"We have lots of rain, Toon . . . few days on the land. When you work so little, you spend more time here, ja?" Again, she laughed with attempted levity, drawing a similar response from her husband.

"We start again tomorrow, though." He looked at her and continued, "Tomorrow will begin many days of warmth. It will be summer soon."

"Ja, Toon," she said as she sat across the table, her cup next to his.

"Tryntje," he said, reaching for her hand, "we must start over tomorrow."

She looked at him strangely.

"Ja, tomorrow we start again . . . in the sun," she said again.

"Tomorrow we start over, *lieveling*."

His smile faded as his eyes focused on her. They seemed to reach for her and hold her, bracing her from a fall.

"*Wat zeg je nou?*"

"The rain, Tryntje; it washed out the seed. The water ran through the ground, carrying the seed along to the bottom of the land." His right arm snaked through the air, mimicking the movement.

Her set smile faded in a moment. She felt the *modder* between her fingers and saw the thick black dirt under her fingernails. And he felt it too. Fifteen years of marriage had brought them so close that no pretense was opaque enough to hide reality. She rose quickly from the table; he saw her trying to restrain her reaction.

"I think that it will be good," she said, taking the cups from the table, "but I do not want to tell the children."

He saw the signs of weariness in her eyes. She refused to look at him, not out of anger, but because she knew her eyes would speak too much. Instead, she made herself busy about the stove, preparing corn bread for tomorrow's meals.

"I know this is not good news, Tryntje; I am not happy myself, for I would do the work of oxen to keep you and the children from the land."

"Now, Antonie, you know that we must help. It is part of our responsibility. The children are getting older. We all have strong backs — thick legs, we can do what we must..."

"You are a good woman, *moeder*," he broke in softly. His eyes followed the soft lines of her body as she worked, from her light shoulders through her waist, grown thinner since they had come here. He had seen her widen at the hips, bearing five children. But her legs were thin and weak. She was not made for this, he knew. Many had wanted her in Vroomshoop; he was blessed to have her for his wife. How it hurt him to see her plodding through the dirt, her back bent to the earth like a slave before its master, following their boy, Hendrick, as he dropped the seed into the furrows. Her hands were rough and blistered from the hoe, even today.

"Tryntje," he said.

"Ja." She still didn't face him.

"Someday I will give you what you deserve. The Lord will bless us, my wife, I know He will. He is faithful to those who love Him."

She grabbed another tightly-wound bundle of prairie grass and threw it into the stove, closing her eyes to everything. She had to tell about her signs, but she could not tell him now.

The sun, hidden throughout the day, dropped below the

horizon, and the moon, like a replacement, poured its silver light over the wet grasses. The three Vander Meer children came in from their work, laughing, They, too, had seen the sun and the sky. They, too, knew that the next morning would be full of promise.

The sun gleamed like an armored hero the next morning. Bright and warm, it conjured little whiffs of steam from the broken ground of the Vander Meer homestead and lofted them up into the atmosphere, where they quickly disappeared. By noon, however, the sun glared upon the prairie, drying the skin of the topsoil quickly, and turning the chunks of upturned sod from shiny black to coarse gray.

Antonie Vander Meer started working at noon. He harnessed his team to the plow, set the shining steel into the untouched earth, and spoke calmly to the horses. They responded grudgingly, but jerked forward, pulling the share through the reddened grasses that had been chopped short earlier in the month. The ground ripped like cloth, and a dark black roll of mud slid cleanly up the share, then curled back and flopped to the stubbled grass, leaving the shiny-smooth loam exposed to the heavens.

Vander Meer loved this moment, for while he felt a certain reluctance toward this violation of the land, he knew his task was significant. The rich earth, loose and clean, smelled of life. It was to be his heritage, the progenitor of a new life, a new land, for his family, for his people. To him this was not work, it was his call. As his team jerked the share deeply through the earth, he saw a farm here, and a neat, white, frame house in the middle, circled by a grove of trees, cottonwoods perhaps. This land, with the grace of the Lord, would bring him and others like him, good Hollanders, into that dream; it would bring his wife comfort, his children education and happiness. And when the rows of corn would sweep like tight ropes across the broken ground, when regiments of golden tassles would float in the wind, this land itself would glorify the Lord.

All day Antonie Vander Meer worked in the field, alone. It was too wet to replant the corn, so Peter and Hendrick pulled the roots from the cut soil and gathered them into piles, while Maria, his daughter, wound some into tight bundles to replenish the supply for the stove. Tryntje stayed in the house, working constantly to clean up the mud from the storm, wash clothing, prepare the meals.

"Tomorrow," Antonie said after supper, "tomorrow we must seed again." The ground would be drier then, dry enough to use the harrow. The children sat silent. Only a week ago they had finally thought themselves finished; now they had to start again.

"How long will it be?" Peter asked.

"Three, maybe four days," his father answered. "I have broken more ground today, but what we've already done will not be hard to do again."

"Early, then, father?"

"Ja. early."

Tryntje was up before the sun, getting things in order for the long days ahead. Not even Maria was excused from the work; she would help her father by standing on the harrow to make it dig more deeply into the soil. Or, like yesterday, she could pull the grass roots out of the sod and gather them in piles, either to be wound into bundles or burned. She would be kept busy, like all the rest.

Tryntje turned down the lantern when the sun broke through the crude window cut into the "prairie logs" on the east wall. She sliced the pork into rations, planning the day's meals. Still she had had no sign. She had borne five children, one dead at birth, so she knew about these things, and as each day passed, she was more sure. She must tell her husband. The three children still slept soundly against the south wall of the cabin. Her husband had been up even before her that morning.

She leaned over the makeshift table, lifting the table cloth to select the eating utensils from the inside of the box. Then she knew it. Her stomach seemed to jump and turn. But she swallowed deeply, holding her sickness in. She put water on the stove for her husband, never stopping the preparations for the day.

Not long after breakfast the work began. It went slower than

Vander Meer had hoped, for the moisture had not left the soil, and when the spikes of the harrow dug into the earth, thick clods formed quickly between the teeth, forcing Antonie to stop frequently and clean off the mud. Roots, still lodged in the soil, were as much of a problem; they jammed against the spikes, forcing the entire harrow to skid uselessly on the surface. Hendrick helped his father then by scraping and cleaning the harrow, while his father, back and leg muscles straining, lifted and held the implement completely clear of the ground. When Antonie saw Hendrick's boots caked with mud, he realized that every member of his family had carried this additional burden through the field. He scarcely noticed his own feet.

The harrow smoothed over the rain-furrowed land. Because he was forced to work slowly, the entire planting operation was bogged down. Peter followed the harrow, digging little cones in the soil with a hoe. Then came Hendrick, swathed by a thick belt of seed corn rolled into his mother's old apron, dropping only three or four kernels into each of the openings. Finally, their mother, also armed with a hoe, tramped through the dirt, covering what had just been deposited in the soil. Maria flitted about, chirping like a red-winged blackbird, helping here and there, and constantly reminding her father of the unusual stream of light smoke that rose daily in the southwest. Vander Meer told her he would investigate, and her curiosity diminished.

And so they worked, breaking off only at noon, as much to rest as to eat. As the day wore on, the sun dried the deeper earth, allowing the harrow to pulverize the flattened soil more efficiently. The brigade of Vander Meer husbandmen moved at a quicker pace.

Antonie never stopped, even for dinner. Tryntje gave him some pieces of corn bread and pork, but he continued to trudge behind the young team of horses, pulling out in front of the rest of the family. By supper his calf muscles were as hard as melons, and his knees were weak, for the harrow moved easily over the dirt in the afternoon, forcing him to dig his heels into the soft earth to brake the pace of his team.

Tryntje could move no more by suppertime. She and Hendrick gave up their field work for the day, while Antonie and Peter harnessed the team to plow again and broke more prairie. By the time the sun had set, a wide new swath of loam lay turned out of its centuries-old resting place.

But Tryntje went to bed early. Her back was cramped by strain; it burned from her buttocks to her shoulders. Her hands were raw from the hoe handle. Even a week of callouses couldn't prevent the slivvery wood from working through to the soft flesh underneath. The sun had turned her neck an angry red again. She had sipped her coffee slowly that night, wondering from where she could draw strength for the continuing assault.

She prayed, though, in spite of her hopelessness. She asked for a blessing, expecting nothing, feeling that no one was there. The dead cottonwood, standing alone in the bleak expanse of grassland, seemed more real, more omnipotent than the God she thought she knew. Surely He had lost them here.

And yet the work continued, for dawn signalled another day, then another, and another. The harder the family worked, she thought, the more fanatically her husband plowed, opening up more and more land to be planted. Each day she worried about her failing strength, and each day she saw her children, subdued by their own exhaustion, sitting around the shipping crate like old people, their faces scraped and scoured by the fiery sun and the searing prairie winds. They should have been in school, she told herself. In Holland they would be clean and nicely dressed. At night they would learn their lessons: spelling, writing, music, history, poetry. They would read Huygens and Da Costa, and sleep well in soft beds built from wood, not sod and straw. She hated this land!

And each night her husband would return, tired and sore himself, wearing a hesitant smile that begged her to share his enthusiasm, while it offered sympathy. They would lie together at night, close to their children, his heavy hand resting on her side as she faced away from him, too exhausted to sleep. They would lie in that position for hours, silent but awake, separated by a wall of fatigue and emotion, listening to the crackle of straw beneath the bodies of their overtired children. In those agonizing hours, Tryntje would remember the thump of the hammer and the rip of the saw as the coffin-maker prepared the little box for her tiny daughter. They had lost her in Minnesota, the cause still a mystery. And now, when she felt a new life beginning to form within her, she wanted to cry out in anguish because this one would know only a vast, dismal ocean of grass.

"Tryntje," her husband said late one night, "are you awake?"

"Ja, Toon."

"We have but a little left now. One, maybe two days."

"That is good," she said, remaining very still.

"We have done well."

"Ja, we have."

"We have more land planted than I thought." He wanted to act as hopeful as possible.

But there was no reply.

"If the Lord gives us a good year . . ."

"Toon . . ." she interrupted.

"Ja?"

She said nothing. Maria turned in her sleep, breaking the silence. Then it was quiet again.

"Toon, I will have a child."

"Oh, *lieveling* . . ."

"Please, say nothing."

"But, Tryntje . . ."

"Please," she stopped him again.

Again silence.

"Tryntje, the Lord . . ."

"Antonie, I know what you must say . . . Please?"

He said no more.

Late Friday afternoon Antonie Vander Meer worked alone, planting the seeds and covering them himself. He had little left to do, so he sent his family back to the sod house to finish the day away from field work. For the first time since they had started on Tuesday, he saw their faces brighten when they sensed the end coming. He sent Tryntje home first with Maria, then Hendrick and Peter. By tonight he would be done, but tomorrow he should work a garden for Tryntje, or mend the leaks in the thatched roof. The week had been good for him. The Lord had blessed him and his family with five clear, bright days of growing weather, enough warmth, certainly, to send young green shoots budding from the seeds. He removed his hat, dropped it over the handle of the hoe, then placed both hands over it, and gave thanks for God's goodness. He asked for mercy for Tryntje, too, and strength for her and their children, all of them.

Then he looked up to the east and south, tracing the lines of his land by erecting the fences in his mind. Peter would help him, of course. Once the crop was growing well, they could start to fence in the farm—Peter would like that work. He followed the limits west, stopping at the big cottonwood, then moved back north toward the sod house. As his eyes swept over his little kingdom, he saw them—huge, billowing monsters rolling from the west, ready at any moment to swallow the sun behind a blanket of bluish-gray. The rain was coming again.

And somehow he had sensed it all day. He had seen the whiskery morning clouds evolve into harmless puffs in the early afternoon. He remembered the relief he had felt when the sun was eclipsed. But he had not dared to acknowledge what would happen.

There was little doubt now. Cold air seemed to ride the back of the clouds, for when the sun finally disappeared behind the ominous bank, Vander Meer's sweat turned icy in the northern wind. All around, the prairie grass, blown in masses by the stiff, cold breezes, moved up and back, spasmodically, like the hide of a cat. It was obvious to him that he could not finish. He threw the hoe over his shoulder and started walking back to the house, watching jagged branches of lightning play in the darkening sky, still far away.

By the time he arrived at the house, Tryntje had already lit the lamps. The three children were inside. Hendrick and Maria read quietly from two of the few books the family owned. Peter stared out of the window to the south, while Tryntje was busy over the stove. No one spoke.

"We have worked hard," he said, hanging up his hat. "The Lord will bless us."

Peter turned quickly, his youthful face agitated by what he saw approaching. He sat down at the table, next to his father.

"The work is finished. Next week we can start to fence, Peter.

The work will not be easy, but it will be good work. Soon our land will be marked to every corner." Antonie tried to distract his son, but the deep rumble of distant thunder was too easily heard and felt in the background.

Tryntje kept working. She didn't respond to her husband. The darkness swept into the house as the storm clouds approached the homestead. She turned up the lamps, and served coffee to Peter and Antonie.

"Sunday we will walk, Tryntje, all of us, to where Maria saw the smoke in the south. We must have neighbors there, eh, Peter?"

"I thought no one lived to the south, Vader."

"Ja, so did I. But we will meet them on Sunday."

"Do you think they are Hollanders?"

"It seems too far from Orange City. Boschma said no one lived here when we took the land. We will find out this Sunday."

Peter looked up suddenly and ran to the window. Tryntje and Antonie heard it too, like a thousand little animals running together over the earth.

"The Lord will bless us," Antonie said again, quietly, to no one but himself.

Then the rains came.

Unlike the week before, the new storm was scattered and sporadic. The rain came in spurts, but water soaked through the bundles of prairie grass that lay like a mat on the roof. It slowly seeped through the ceiling, dripping finally onto the dirt floor, turning Tryntje's home into a muddy den once more.

By Saturday night Hendrick and Maria had paged through every book, and all the coffee was gone. Other than the clatter of a frequent cloudburst, there was little noise within the thick mud walls. Peter and Antonie had gone out periodically to feed the animals in the lean-to behind the house, while Tryntje had found plenty of work inside, mending and sewing.

All this seemed another curse to Tryntje, but she didn't complain. The new life within her was the source of much anxiety, but it helped her push forward as well. When the soggy blankets and high humidity provoked a chill, she would wrap a hot brick from the stove and put it next to her feet, or even put on more clothes—not for herself, but for the baby. She watched herself closely, and in the process, the despair prompted by her environment settled into the recesses of her mind—still present, but for the moment subordinate to her instinct as mother. This new attitude caused no change in her behavior, however, for her new concern dominated her activity with equal intensity, and whatever strength she did not expend on her children was absorbed by the infant she was already able to see before her.

Even Antonie saw nothing of the change. Her solemnity, her quietness, he felt to be the product of her covert distaste for the new land. And as the beating rain continued to blanket the earth, he felt his faith begin to ebb in the stream of tribulations he suffered as father, husband, and believer.

"I can take no more," he silently told the Lord. "Please bring us deliverance!"

But the rain fell persistently. Antonie and Tryntje lay motionless on the bedding, hearing every drop, while feeling the dampness invade the sod house again. Antonie stared into the darkness and groped for ways to accept this seeming curse.

Then he rose silently, slipped across the muddied floor, grabbed his coat and hat from the nail at the door, and left the house. He ran over the slick earth as fast as he dared until he reached the field—the first field he had plowed, the one that sloped slightly toward the bog. He raged at his stupidity. He knew he should not have chosen this land first. It had already shed the first planting; now more rain threatened a repetition that could destroy the productive farm he had envisioned, and even his faith in a loving God.

The rain continued falling. It smacked into his hat and ran down around the brim where it dropped steadily, forming a kind of fringe. The land was already scarred by tiny rivulets beginning to connect with each other. Streams of water ate into the earth, carrying topsoil down toward the slough. In the face of the infinite black sky he felt powerless. He was driven back to his knees, like a child, staring at the jagged crevices in his land until his eyes closed in another prayer—short, almost inarticulate, but burdened with all he had ever been, all he ever wanted to be.

Then he asked God's blessing on his last frail hope, stood up, threw off his coat, despite the cold, and rolled up his shirt sleeves as he stepped into the muck. He could barely distinguish the little mounds where seeds had been planted, but he tried to adjust his position to leave the seed undisturbed. He leaned over, buried his hand in the warm earth, and felt the wet mud strangle his fingers. He closed his hand into a cup like a swimmer, dug out a scoop of mushy soil, and laid it beside the hole, taking a step forward. Soon, a thin furrow traversed the slope, collecting the runoff as it moved slowly downward. For hours he worked, until his field was ribboned by jagged lines. His fingers were cleaned by the soil, but the heel of his palm and his wrists were blackened by dirt.

He stood and surveyed his work. The rain continued to fall, but it ran into the troughs he had dug with his hands . . . .

Tryntje was awake when he returned, but Antonie laid his drenched body next to her without speaking, listening, like her, to the drops, unable to hear whether there might be any diminution. All that mattered now was how long this continued.

The grass roof, saturated again by more than a day of rain, continued to drip long after the storm had passed. Not until he rose from the straw bed once more and stepped outside was he sure. It was over.

Even Tryntje sensed the relief and joy in the rhythmical throbbing of the psalms that Sunday morning. The sun had appeared again, and when Antonie returned from an early walk, his face broadened by a real smile, she felt a twinge of the enthusiasm that her husband seemed almost always to possess. He told them of the fields — very little had been washed away. So with another breakfast over, the sun drying the land again, and no threat of reseeding, the family found a relaxed and happy intimacy in their Sabbath worship. Antonie led even more songs than usual, prayed even longer, and read more lustily from the stories of the Old Testament. His joy was bounded only by the absence of a larger fellowship.

"We will start another sod house this summer," he told Peter after their worship.

"Another?"

"Ja, we must build a house of worship for our God." He saw his family, clean and refreshed, in a good church building, singing the psalms, listening to the Dominie, worshiping with the greater family of God. And all around him would be other Dutch people who would follow the Vander Meers to this place, Christian people, who, like him, would thank their God for His blessings. Tryntje heard his words to Peter. She looked up at the family portrait, longing to share her husband's vision. And she smiled, then, and poured her husband some of her home-brewed prairie tea, made from some dried grasses her husband had collected for her.

After dinner the entire family stood beside the house, staring south, looking for the faint thread of smoke that Maria had pointed out to them on other days. But today there was no sign. Before them lay the sage grass, waving in a mellow southern breeze. It rolled like ocean swells far, far into the south; but they saw no signs of other humans.

"Maybe we stay home, Tryntje. I see nothing today," he told his wife. He himself had lost his direction in the grass several times, and he was reluctant to take such chances with his whole family.

"No, Vader, I will show you."

He smiled at his pretty daughter. She was clean and neat. Of course, his wife had seen to that. No matter how muddy things became, no matter how wet, Tryntje always kept Maria clean and dry. She had already lost one daughter.

"Let's go, Vader! We've never been farther than the sod-pile by the old cottonwood." Peter was not to be denied.

"We will stay together. We promise, Vader!" Hendrick put in. He looked into his mother's eyes and scampered toward the south, beckoning them to follow. Antonie also looked into his wife's eyes to get her permission. Her stiff, dry hair blew softly in the breeze.

"Can you, Vrouw?"

"Ja." She smiled.

"Very well. We go."

Once they were past the limits of their own claim, they felt like adventurers, even though there was clearly nothing in the area besides the prairie grass. But, at times, the ground bottomed into soggy sloughs, and in order to find alternative routes, Antonie made them all hold hands as they passed through grass that grew higher than his head. Then they would scale a slight rise, and the grass would shorten. Suspicious blackbirds screamed raspy warnings, and small bands of prairie pigeons flew close to their heads, their wings thumping like little drums against their bellies. Hendrick said that he spotted a badger, but by the time the others looked, it was gone.

Still they pressed on to the south. Miles passed as they moved up the knolls and through the hollows. Then they saw it, suddenly, as they reached the crest of another hill. A real frame cabin, standing alone on a small incline. There was no fire just then, but even from a distance, beaten paths were visible, signs of life were there. The grass was cut shorter around the house, and a wide strip of plowed land ran along the top of the knoll.

"I knew we would find it!" Maria shouted, jumping happily and infecting the others with her excitement.

"Maybe they will help us build the church, Vader." Peter had not forgotten his father's words.

They approached the cabin slowly but with great hope. The children seemed to want to hide behind their parents; even Peter walked behind his father, peeking around his wide shoulders.

Then the door of the cabin opened, and a woman backed out, latching the door. The Vander Meers stopped walking immediately, watching her. She turned, grasped the bottom of the wooden pail she was carrying, and dumped the contents onto the stubbly grass. As she finished, she glanced up and froze, confronted by this new and unexpected tribe.

"Hul-lo," Antonie stumbled over the little English he knew.

There was no reply. The woman stood motionless, still holding the pail upside down. She was entranced by Tryntje, it seemed; at least she appeared to pay little attention to the rest of the family. Antonie looked at his wife. She, in turn, seemed transfixed by the woman who stared at her.

"Dina," Tryntje whispered.

"Dina?" she repeated, more loudly.

"Tryntje?" The woman's round face lengthened as she gaped in disbelief.

Both women drew their long skirts up from the ground and ran toward each other, then stopped at arm's length, incredulous, holding hands and studying each other closely, with obvious delight.

Antonie heard very little of their conversation, but when the women embraced and kissed, he knew he had been blessed.

Tryntje turned back to her family, her lips in constant motion, her left arm still embracing the stranger. She waved her family forward with a girlish swoop of her right hand.

"This is Dina . . . my friend . . .," she said, her face as warm as the morning sun, "from Holland . . . the singing school!"

The two women turned back into each other's arms, as five children, one after the other, exploded from the cabin door and ran to their mother, while watching the Vander Meer children closely. Then a tall, gaunt Hollander filled the door frame and looked suspiciously at the emotional reunion taking place before his home. When he saw the look on his wife's face, he glanced over to Antonie Vander Meer, who nodded and smiled.

As the sun inched closer to the horizon that night, Antonie and his family finally reached their southwest sod-pile. Peter had gone ahead of the rest, and when they caught up with him, he was sitting on the marker, one hand holding the big sack of coffee, the other shading the bright sun from his eyes as he looked into the west. Tryntje held Maria's hand, while Antonie walked arm and arm with his wife on the other side.

"Vader, look!" Peter pointed upward through the branches of the old cottonwood, and there, like fancy lace against the orange sky, a huge regiment of geese—three, four, five echelons—moved north in formation. The Vander Meers stopped there at the corner of their land and watched the geese, listening and laughing at the discordant honking.

"Vader, is it true what they say about the geese?" Peter asked.

"What is that?"

"The ones in front get tired," he said pointing toward the little specks in the northwest sky. "They slow down and drop to the rear. Then others lead. That way they can keep going."

They all watched the formation, perfect now in its distant perspective.

"A man in Minnesota told me so, but I didn't see them change. Is it true?"

Antonie laughed as he watched the geese disappear into the heavens.

"I don't know, son, but, ja, it probably is. Our God is theirs too."

He lifted his arm and circled Tryntje's shoulder, pulling her close. Together they walked back to their sod home, the children following.

Questions for Reflection and Discussion:

1. Contrast Tryntje's view of the landscape and the sky with her husband's view as the story begins.
2. Why does Tryntje think about her homeland so often?
3. How does the author use the dead cottonwood as a symbol?
4. Point out several well-constructed similes. What is their tonal effect?
5. What is the meaning of the troughs that Antonie digs with his hands?
6. What are several of the "signs" suggested by the title?
7. Interpret the final scene, with its dialogue on the geese.

JAMES SCHAAP

Through Devious Ways

John had seen the broken chain lying like a bull snake on the bed of the wagon when the raw frost still gloved the leaves of the yellowed corn. He didn't mention it when De Regt had given him explicit instructions about the husking, because he knew the man, or at least his father did. After all, he told himself, Hermanus and his wife had coffee with the Van der Walls nearly every Sunday between the services at the church in Prinsburg. He just assumed De Regt had also noticed the chain and would fix it as soon as possible.

So he started snapping ears from the stalks and tossing them blindly off the bangboard and into the wagon. It had still been dark when De Regt left the field; the sun had only begun to lighten the eastern sky. A few down ears, covered by dirt and stuck by frost, made John's work more tedious, but De Regt was a proper farmer—he knew when to harvest his corn. The stalks stood high and proud in straight rows.

And John was proud of his abilities. He had acquired a reputation among the farmers for being a tireless and efficient worker. Many jobs were offered him during the harvest season. The frozen ears, the down ears, were all part of his job, and although their stubbornness wore at his nerves and fingers, he never thought of complaining, for he had picked corn in many fields more ragged than this one.

De Regt had left his son behind to pick the down rows. Henry was nearly thirteen, Hermanus' oldest boy, and he, too, worked hard to clean the ears from his row. But when dawn warmed into morning, when the sun quilted the Minnesota soil, melting the frost from the rows, Henry's head popped up more frequently from behind the wagon, telling of the boy's weariness, and John would wait, impatiently, to signal the horses to move ahead.

Little more than an hour had passed before John shed his overall jacket and hung it on the wagon. He glanced back and saw the boy chucking clods of mud at a meadow lark perched on a fence post.

"Here, junge!" he commanded.

Henry glanced at him, then threw two more clods before the bird finally flew from its perch.

"Ja, ja. I'm coming. I'm coming," he grumbled.

John stood for a moment, allowing the boy to catch up, and looked into the wagon. Hundreds of nearly clean ears were piled unevenly against the right side, beneath the bangboard, but the bed was still visible near the left wall. Buried already was the chain that should have spanned and secured the sides of the wagon. Hermanus would be back to fix it soon, he told himself. His father always said that Hermanus De Regt was a good farmer.

"Giddap!" he signalled the horses and the work continued. The ripened ears cracked off the stalks easily and cleanly. Hermanus' gloves were old and worn, but John was an experienced picker. He had the right touch. Pull the hook back through the leaves, holding the ear with the left hand; jerk the ear and pull it away with the right, leaving a handful of leaves in the left, and toss it off the bangboard and into the wagon—all in one smooth motion. He had been at it for years, doing a man's share long before he was fourteen. He could barely remember picking the inside rows. On almost any day he could pick a hundred bushels.

The ears banged off the board—"clunk," "clunk," "clunk"—evenly, almost mechanically.

By mid-morning his fingers and wrists were loose and supple, warmed by the October sun and the constant jerking motion. He remembered other jobs when stubborn ears would stick to the stalks as if nailed there. Regular jerking wouldn't break them, and pain would flow through his hand and arm, and his wrist would pull itself out of joint. The pain would be so bad that he would be forced to quit; his wrists would swell as if they were infected. The Van der Walls couldn't afford any lost time this harvest. His father counted on the money that John made picking corn.

When the sun stood nearly above his head, John Van der Wall noticed Hermanus returning to the field, straight as a poplar. By then the wagon seemed almost filled, its sides bulging abnormally. De Regt cut through the field behind them, retracing the path of the wagon. The team moved forward on command, and the work continued, but John saw his employer emerge from the corn with a handful of ears and lay them down where John could reach them when the wagon passed that way again. De Regt continued cleaning up until he reached his son, some ten yards behind the wagon. Their muffled voices were barely audible over the snapping ears and the slow drone of the wind through the rows.

De Regt was tall and gaunt with a bony face and a long, Indian-like nose that arched from between two bulging eyes. His head seemed to bob like a crow's when he stepped carefully between the corn. His lips curled downward beneath a light moustache that grew like wild thistles down around the corners of his mouth, and his unkempt hair hung in little clumps around his ears. John remembered having once thought that De Regt looked like the portrait of George Washington that hung in the bank at Prinsburg.

When he reached John, De Regt turned and looked down the rows that ran straight as a taut rope. "How is the boy doing, John?" he asked.

"Good."

"Ja, he is a good worker."

John glanced back at Henry De Regt. The boy was barely visible, his back arched to the earth where he cleaned the ears from the inside row.

"You should get them all, John. Look at the piles I've picked there." He pointed a bony finger. "You're no child anymore—we can't just forgive such carelessness."

"Ja, I'll try." John continued to pick, looking up only when spoken to.

"Good day for husking here, ja?" De Regt removed his cap and brushed back his thin graying hair. "The sunshine's warm, but the breeze is cool. And the field is dry."

"Ja, it is a good day." John looked up at his employer. There was a white ring about his forehead where the cap usually sat; otherwise, his face was as brown as the soil of his farm.

"Well, you are getting a load here, eh?"

"Ja, I think it is full. Do you want—"

"Oh, no, no, no. Plenty more will go in here yet. I can barely see the load above the box."

John stopped, surprised, but said nothing.

"No, you can get more on yet. I must fix the fence here. It is almost noon. I'll tell you when it is full. You can easily get in the rest of the row here." He pointed down the field, not even waiting for any response. He took three big steps back to the inside row, said something to his son again, and moved away.

"Mr. De Regt!" John could not let it pass so easily.

"Ja?" He turned back, his straight face above the corn, eyelids drooping over his swollen eyes.

"The wagon. You know about it?"

"What's that?"

"I say, the wagon, you know?"

"Ja, what of the wagon?"

"The chain is busted."

"Eh?"

"The chain—"

"Ach, ja, the chain . . . I forgot to fix it. Ja, sure. I will fix it. Sure, sure, sure!" He waved impatiently, turned, and left.

John looked at the wagon. The sides were bulging from the weight of the ears. He knew the wagon was full. But his father knew Hermanus De Regt. They had gone to the same church for as long as John Van der Wall could remember.

By the time he pulled the husking hook over his right glove again, he was angry. He had unloaded the entire wagon by himself—even the boy had not helped—and he was sure it held more than thirty bushels. Scooping out the load was hard work; it always was, hardly a relief from the monotonous hours of picking. But a sense of injustice kindled some new emotion within John Van der Wall, and his scoop worked constantly, even easily, moved by rising annoyance. When the box was empty, he looked again at the bin and was convinced that he was right.

Hermanus De Regt was still nowhere around. The boy bounded from the house when he saw the wagon empty, and vaulted into the box, picking up the reins on the way.

"Let's go, John. I'll drive."

"Where is your father?"

"I don't know." The boy seemed impatient.

John stood in the empty wagon, holding the broken chain. He scanned the entire yard, but nowhere did he see the man.

"Come on, John! We have to get another load!"

John nodded, and the horses jerked the wagon forward, back to the cornfield.

De Regt's gloves were already reversed from many hours of work. The morning's husking had opened holes in the fingers, and John's nails soon wore down from the work. The balls of his fingers became tender, and each snapping ear sent pain searing through his hand. In the heat of his irritation, pain and exhaustion turned to bitterness. Angered, sullen, he felt only injustice.

But it made him work even harder. He became so swollen by his sense of outrage that the ears seemed to drop from the stalks. He picked faster and harder, exasperated by Henry when the boy couldn't keep up, but helping with the inside row to keep the wagon moving over the soft earth.

"Ja, John, you are doing better. I find only a few ears in the rows."

He looked up quickly, surprised to see De Regt standing before him. He hadn't seen him approach.

"Are you thirsty?"

"No, sir." John kept working, the hard ears clunking off the bangboard.

De Regt said no more. He turned to his son and helped with his row. In a few minutes they were nearly at the back of the wagon. John moved even faster in order to keep ahead. Soon the sides of the wagon were bulging again, the wood curving like a buggy spring. But Hermanus kept working, talking occasionally to his son. John said nothing this time, his anger fomenting into hatred, his lips sealed by stubbornness.

"Hey, John, stop once!"

He heard the command and stood waiting like a tortured slave, his back to the master.

"You take all the rows down the field to the end there, ja? I need Henry to fix the fence. When you get to the end, take the load and put it in the crib. Then you can meet us back here."

John turned slowly to face his employer. The wagon was already full. He wanted to shout at the man, to tell him again about the chain, to scream about the full load, to remind him of Cornelius Van der Wall, his father, but his own stubborn hatred grew into a vicious delight in the injustice he felt himself suffering. He said nothing, but nodded slowly and turned back to the field.

In a moment father and son were gone and John was left to take all three rows. When he finally came to the end of the field, the load was heaped into a steep hill. Over 35 bushels, for sure.

When he returned to the field, John knew that suppertime was passing. The sun had fallen into the western sky, and the breezes which had kept the work cool through the morning and afternoon began to chill. Hermanus and his son awaited him at the point where he was to begin. He pulled the horses into the proper row and tied the reins securely, saying nothing.

"You work hard, John. Your father should be proud. You unloaded nearly 30 bushels faster than most men could."

John tightened his swollen hands into fists for a moment to control his rage. There hadn't been an ear less than 35. He pulled his overall jacket on once more, stepped into his rows, and began to pick again, accelerating the pace he had set earlier.

"John!"

He stopped and faced De Regt.

"Henry says he'll work until it gets dark and then have his supper. Is that good with you?"

"Yes, sir."

Hermanus left then, but he returned when darkness fell over

the fields. Nearly a half load was already piled in the wagon, covering the broken chain again.

"Ja, boys, it's a good day's work," he said, hands on hips. "But it's time to stop now." He walked over to the wagon as both Henry and John began to remove their tattered gloves. "Thirty and 30 plus what's here. Ja, 14 or 15? That's 75 bushels. Good work, eh, John?"

John threw the gloves into the box and jumped in himself. "Not so good, Hermanus. I've done much better."

"Better?" De Regt looked almost surprised.

"Ja, much better."

"Ach, 75 bushels is a good day's work for a boy like you. Not even some men can pick that much."

De Regt stood by his son, who drove the team back from the field.

In an hour John Van der Wall was home. Hermanus De Regt had invited him to stay for supper with his family, but John had quietly insisted that he would prefer to eat at home. As an after-thought, De Regt promised to have the wagon fixed by the next morning.

John told his parents nothing about what had happened, ate very little, and went directly to bed. It was late, and tomorrow would be early again. He lay awake, quiet, sullen, his body tired, his fingers numb, his mind wrenched between two images of Hermanus De Regt, his own and that of his father. He made no resolutions, no decisions about tomorrow, for he still believed that De Regt was a man of his word. His body, like his mind, seemed unsettled, for when he finally slept, he rolled on his bed as if he were sleeping on gravel.

"Morning, John."

The cold October air seeped through his jacket like water, but the frigid hour's walk was forgotten in a moment when he saw his employer.

"Morning."

"Well, let's get started. Two more days like yesterday and we might have it all in."

John walked slowly to the wagon and glanced over the side. The chain was still broken, buried beneath the corn picked late last night.

"What about the chain, Hermanus?"

"Eh?"

"I said, what about the chain?"

"Ach, ja, ja. I forgot about it." He snapped his fingers impulsively. "I will get at it today, sure."

"*Now*, De Regt." John stood, looking straight at the taller Hermanus.

"What is that?"

"I said, fix it now, or I don't work."

The wind rushed through the corn. The men looked into each other's eyes.

"No! Get to work, Van der Wall." De Regt's eyes bulged with amazement.

"I will not work until the wagon is fixed. If you want me to work, fix the wagon."

"Why, your father, John—"

"My father isn't working here. *I* am your hired man. But I will quit—now—if you don't fix the wagon."

"But why? Surely you don't—"

"I picked more than 75 bushels yesterday, De Regt, much more. You are not being fair with me."

De Regt rubbed his eyes nervously, saying nothing. He looked back at the morning sky to the east, then surveyed the remainder of his corn. Finally he stared back at his employee, looking stern and almost fatherly.

"I say you will work, Johannes."

Henry stood quietly at his father's side. His eyes moved uncertainly from the man at his left to John Van der Wall.

"I say you will go to work now, Johannes Van der Wall." De Regt lightened his tone, conscious of the boy at his side.

"I mean no disrespect, Hermanus. I just want what is fair." John's resolution gained strength in the confrontation. A full day of what-ought-not-to-be reinforced his belief in what he was doing now.

"I am the boss here." Hermanus put his hands on his waist.

"You are here because I hired you. I will determine what is fair, what is just. How dare you?"

Henry stepped over to the inside row; dry corn stalks cracked as he walked.

"Well? Go to work!"

"When you fix the wagon, De Regt."

De Regt leaned over slowly and jerked at a broken stalk, then peeled the leaves slowly away. He glanced at his son.

"Very well then, you may go. I will find someone else in your place."

John walked down the field, his face lit by a small, unflinching smile.

"—and there are many other, Johannes!" De Regt yelled. "There are many others who need to work, who need the money. Your father knows that, too."

John Van der Wall didn't stop to listen, but he heard each word clearly as he marched down the row toward the gate.

His tracks were still fresh across the dew on the forty acres of pasture that he crossed to reach De Regt's farm. The sun rose in a blaze as he walked east across the meadow, face lifted. He stopped for a moment and stripped the overall jacket from his shoulders. He straightened it carefully, holding it by the collar. He had paid nearly a dollar for it in Willmar. His own money. Pa couldn't afford it, he knew. He threw it back over his shoulder, still holding the collar, and kept walking.

He was sure he could get another husking job. Ben McCrory had talked to him just last week. Pa hadn't been able to afford much the last two years. Almost everything John needed for work was from his own earnings. Even some of his little brother's things—shoes, a cap—were bought with his money.

Almost two years ago, he remembered, the crops had looked tall and strong in early July. The corn stood more than waist high. His father had thanked the Lord as he asked His blessing every mealtime, it seemed. They had bought ten more acres four years ago, and John understood that a good crop would keep the creditors happy for at least another year. And then the hail. One night it was hot, hot and wet when they settled into their bunks.

But the wind, a slashing wind that shrieked through the elm grove, lightning that made the yard as light as day, and thunder that shook the house, woke them all, and sent them into the storm cellar for at least an hour. John remembered his mother praying. And when they came out, little cone-shaped piles stood by the downspouts, like little piles of salt. His father went to his field then, even though it was dark. John remembered seeing his dark figure melt into the night, as the sky flickered with lightning many miles to the east.

John walked through the field of corn where the Van der Wall's hope had stood so high just two years ago. Pa had had to take a job then, with an implement dealer in Raymond. Everyone had been forced to work much harder since then, especially his father. John respected his father. And when Pa Van der Wall expected more from his son, John tried his best to produce.

Their own corn was ready to be picked, but like everything else for the last two years, it would be done only when there was some extra time. He could start today. His little brother could help.

John Van der Wall was running when he entered the yard from behind the barn. The prospect of doing their own corn, plus the sustaining sense of righteousness he felt from his conflict with De Regt made him eager to begin.

His father had already left for work, and his mother was doing the chores alone when he walked up behind her and took the fork from her hands.

"John, what brings you home?" His mother's round face turned to him, her eyes showing surprise.

"I'm not going to work for De Regt again," he said, shoving hay through the chute.

"Well, why? You aren't done yet?"

"No."

"Well?"

"I quit."

"Why?"

"De Regt was not fair to me, Ma." John stood the fork upright and leaned his arms over the handle. "He did wrong."

She untied the red scarf from her head and used it to wipe the sweat and chaff from her temples. There was anguish in her eyes. John saw it and winced as she spoke. "What do you mean?"

"The wagon was busted . . . the chain was broken. All day he promised to fix it, but he never did. He said I picked 75 bushels. He lied. The wagon held much more than 30, much more! You should have seen the box! The sides bent way out like this—" He made an exaggerated curve with his arm.

"Oh, John!" She brought the scarf to her face again.

"But, Ma, don't you see, it wasn't fair—"

His mother shook her head and exhaled hard.

"You finish the chores, John." She said no more but climbed slowly down the ladder to the main floor of the barn.

John did pick corn that day—all day—he didn't even break for dinner. His mother brought him lunch midway through the afternoon, but she made no mention of their neighbor. John knew that his father would return later; then the whole affair would be reviewed thoroughly.

The Van der Wall's corn was not as easy to pick as De Regt's. It had matured earlier, and the strong fall winds had taken a toll amid the rows. But John worked hard, even harder than yesterday, determined to get close to a hundred bushels in, despite his late start. His little brother Peter helped, but he was young and inexperienced, and John found himself helping with the inside row as often as he had when he worked for De Regt.

His father appeared silently late in the afternoon. There was no mention of the incident; both men knew that conversation would follow later at the supper table. They picked until darkness made the ears difficult to find; then John drove the wagon back to the crib and unloaded, while his father did the chores.

By the time John had cleaned up thoroughly, he was ready for the interrogation. He was surprised when the entire supper hour passed with no mention of his quitting at De Regt's. His father talked about a trip to Clara City that day to set up a self-binding reaper. He talked about some cousins of his, and his face brightened when he told of the huge farms he had seen.

Not until devotions were finished and Peter was gone into the front room was the incident between John and Hermanus De Regt even mentioned.

"Now, John," his father began, as his mother took the dishes from the table, "what is this all about—this business between you and De Regt?"

Both men sipped hot coffee.

"He refused to fix the wagon. I asked him to, and he promised he would, but he didn't—he wouldn't." John felt nervous as his father's deep, brown eyes stared into him.

"What was wrong?"

"The chain was broken."

"Is that all?"

John swallowed the last of his coffee and set the cup back in the saucer.

"Ja."

"Well, I don't think I understand. His machinery is *his* business, John. You just work for him."

"He made me fill the wagon, Pa, fill it to overflowing. Twice the wagon was heaped up full—twice! And I asked him to fix it."

"How much did he pay you?"

"He didn't pay me."

"Then how did you know—"

"He told me I picked only 75 bushels. I know there was more. The wagon held 35 at least, probably 40. I know, Pa, I've picked before!"

Only the steady clink of dirty dishes and saucers interrupted the silence. His mother kept working, but listened closely, he knew.

"So you quit because it wasn't fair?"

"Ja."

His father scratched his temples. "Did you think of his side of it?"

"Pa, I asked him more than once—"

"He has to get his crop in alone now."

"He says he can get someone else easy."

John held his head high. His father called to his wife for more coffee.

"Ja, he's right, you know. Lots of boys your age are looking for work. Someone else will just make the money now."

"Pa, would you have kept working if you knew it wasn't fair?"

Cornelius Van der Wall shook his head. "Johannes, Johannes, when the Lord sent the hail—not to Raymond, not to Clara City, not even to De Regt's fields, was He *fair?* Was that *just* of Him?" with such injustice'?"
with such injustice?' "

John looked away. His mother offered him more coffee, but he shook his head.

"When Verburg pays me two dollars for a job that he makes twenty on, do I yell and throw down my wrench? Do I quit and *zannik* about how it's not fair of him?"

John's mother removed her apron and sat down at the table between her husband and her son. She reached out to John as she spoke. "Everything is not always *fair* in this life, John. The Christian knows that, and he must learn to live with it, humbly and prayerfully. Doesn't Paul say too that we must be in subjection to the higher powers?"

"But I can get another job, Pa. McCrory asked me, too, you know. Just last week."

"McCrory is not a church man, John."

"But he is a *good* man, Ma!" John clenched his right hand into a fist. "I would rather work for Ben McCrory than Hermanus De Regt any day."

His father looked up quickly. "You are speaking of a brother in Christ, John!"

John trembled and swallowed quickly. He respected his father's argument, but he was convinced that there was more to all this than his father had yet seen. He laughed lightly, to himself, almost sarcastically, and shook his head. "Hermanus De Regt is no brother of mine. A man who will cheat you on purpose, then lie to you, is no brother of mine."

"John, I'm **sure** he didn't—" his mother tried to appease his anger.

"If he didn't mean it deliberately, Ma, then why didn't he fix the wagon like he promised? It wouldn't take him long."

"I can't answer for Hermanus. He will have to answer for himself." John's father spoke clearly and without emotion. "But you miss the point, John. We who follow Christ must be humble and persevering. 'Blessed are the meek,' He said; 'they shall inherit. . .' But I see no meekness in you. Where is your love and forgiveness?''

John sat silently, looking from his mother to his father.

"It's De Regt who must ask my forgiveness, Pa. He has wronged *me!*'' John had never spoken this way to his parents before, but he was prompted by a vigorous sense of what was right.

His mother looked up cautiously. "Perhaps he should go back tomorrow morning, pa?'' She looked uncertainly at her husband.

"I will not go back, Ma. I told him to fix the wagon or get someone else, and he told me to 'Get to work!' as if I was a slave. I will not be treated like that. I will not work for Hermanus De Regt again.''

Cornelius Van der Wall was silent. Dina was astonished. "We will miss the money, John, you know that.'' She waited for her husband to speak.

"I can get other jobs, Pa.'' John was stronger now. His father's eyes had softened. John had not seen that look on his father's face before, but somehow he understood it, and he felt that he knew he had prevailed. "I'll go to Ben McCrory tomorrow—at lunch,'' he said.

Cornelius nodded his head slowly.

"But, Pa—''

"Ja, Mama, the boy is right. Tomorrow morning he will harvest our corn again, then look for another job.'' He scratched his nose. "But remember what your mother and I have said, Son. You have to learn to take some things. You have to accept the Lord's will, humbly and graciously, even when it is hard. Then you will be blessed, otherwise not.''

"Yes, Pa, I think I understand.''

John rose from the table and went to his room. Through the heating vent he heard his mother crying later, but he heard also the deep, resonant voice of his father. He lay awake on his bed for a long time, confident in victory, but humbled, almost to the point of tears, by a sense of separation which was, to him, both exciting and fearful, and yet but dimly understood.

No one mentioned his quitting until after Sunday dinner several days later. Hermanus and his wife had stopped for coffee after the morning service, as was their custom, but John had no desire to sit around the table with them. He was not missed, however, for he had rarely sat with the adults before. But he knew that his parents would certainly raise the job issue with the neighbors, and he feared that the topic would arise again sometime after the De Regts had left.

Peter left the table quickly after prayer, but rather than begin to clean up the dishes, John's mother sat waiting for what she knew would be a continuation of their earlier discussion.

"Good sermon by the Dominie this morning. Good sermon." His father's observation was obviously intended to provoke a reply.

"What do you think, Son?"

"Ja, it was good." He was surprised at the questioning; his father rarely spoke of the sermon to him, except to reiterate the Dominie's points before Sunday's noon devotions.

"Do you believe what Dominie said?"

"Ja, oh, ja. It was a good sermon."

"And you disagree with nothing?"

The kitchen chair creaked beneath John as he fidgeted, looking desperately for something to add.

"No, I agreed with all that he said."

"Good, good." Cornelius looked stern. John knew that his father had caught him. "Ja, good," he said again. "Dominie spoke of the Lord's control over all things, didn't he?"

John nodded.

"He said that we have to recognize God's hand over us, and do His will—" he pointed to imaginary spots on the table—" in everything we do."

"Ja, but that's not easy," John mouthed familiar words.

"No, that's not. The Lord didn't say it would be."

His father stopped for a moment and lifted his cup. His mother's eyes moved from husband to son and back again.

"Ja," his father drew in a big breath. "Ja, well, we spoke to Hermanus today . . . about you. He said you worked hard." He nodded appreciatively. "He said you were a very good worker."

John breathed more easily for a moment. "Ja, I worked hard. I was angry with him, and I worked very hard."

"Ja, John, he said you were angry, very angry." He stopped again, shook his head slowly and continued. "He said that he fired you because of it."

John's mouth dropped open at his father's words. "He fired me?"

"Ja, Hermanus said he fired you."

"For what?"

"For being angry about the chain, and for swearing at him."

"Swearing?"

"Ja, he says you took the Name of the Lord in vain."

John's mother watched him fearfully. His father's eyes held that strange new softness.

"Ach he lies, Pa."

"John, don't cover up your sin." His mother pointed into his face.

"He says that you damned him with God's Name."

"He lies." John shook his head quickly, a faint smile of disbelief spread across his face.

"Did you, Johannes?" His mother waited.

"Mother, I didn't. I tell you the truth. It all happened like I said."

She cried then, but John didn't know whether her tears were of belief or disbelief.

"I believe you, John." His father's voice was steady. "Hermanus lied, I'm sure of it." He reached over to his wife, pulling her closer to him. She cried softly in short, uneven breaths.

"Ma, go get us some coffee now. I will see De Regt later this afternoon. After church. It will be good, Ma."

She looked up at her son, walked to him and kissed him lightly on the forehead. Then she smiled and left the room.

"Does she believe me, Pa?"

"Ja, John, she believes you, too."

He held out his hand to his father. "Then why does she still cry?"

"For Hermanus."

John sat quietly for a moment, looking at his father. Then he pushed his chair away from the table and rose very slowly. He looked toward the bedroom where his mother had gone, then back to his father.

"John, how goes the work at McCrory's?"

"Good."

"That's good, and the pay?"

"Ja, Pa, good, too—all I need."

John turned away from the table, his mind still possessed by the image of his mother. "Excuse me, Pa?"

"Ja."

Peter bounded into the room just then.

"Time to get ready for church, Peter. We must go now in a little while."

"Ja, Daddy.'"

John was nearly out of the room when he heard his father's voice. "Will you be coming with us, Son?"

John looked back at his father, astonished. The question was new, but it was real. It was in his father's face.

"Ah, ja . . . ja, I will be going." He turned to the stairs, looked back once more at his father and younger brother, and climbed up the stairs to his room.

Questions for Reflection and Discussion:

1. What is the importance of the broken chain?
2. Which are especially significant words in the paragraph of physical description on Hermanus De Regt?
3. What is ironic about the reiteration of Cornelius Van der Wall's estimate of De Regt as a farmer?
4. Why does Cornelius Van der Wall wait until after supper to discuss John's quitting? Discuss the man as a farmer.
5. Who is right in the debate between father and son; and what is "A sense of separation which was, to him [John], both exciting and fearful, and yet but dimly understood"?
6. What does John learn from this experience?
7. What is the meaning of his father's asking whether John will be going to church with the family?

CONTEMPORARY REALISM

Many readers enjoy stories about people who live in other places or who have lived at different times, but there is another large body of readers who prefer fiction that illuminates the situations and concerns of people living today, especially if that vision of contemporary life is an interpretation that provides satisfying answers, or at least gives some measure of hope.

John Updike and Peter De Vries, for example, pretend that happiness can be gained, albeit transitorily, through wit, adultery, and sophisticated cynicism. But the superficiality and hedonism of such fictionists is countered by the darker views of other secularists, such as Kurt Vonnegut, Jr., who says that life is a cat's cradle (a maze of meaningless strings and spaces), and William Golding, who affirms in *Lord of the Flies* that there is something bestial and diabolical deep within man which will explode the "reasonable" dreams of evolutionary idealists. Indeed, some humanists are honest, but only to a point, and usually that untouched point is repentance: the acknowledgement and confession of sin as an affront to God worthy of death.

The six stories in this section are six ways of perceiving, formulating, and telling the truth about the real world of today. "The Artificial Nigger" presents pride, vengefulness, denial, and pardon in the context of an unforgettable grandfather-grandson struggle that works itself out on a pilgrimage journey to the city. God's mercy is the way of reconciliation. "Cracked Wheat" is what Joyce would call an epiphany, an enlightening encounter, in which a young man discovers that his vocation encompasses even his summertime job and that he has been called to represent his Lord in every human relationship, no matter how temporary or inconsequential it may at the time appear.

Walter Lockwood's "Compassion Man" is a delightful satiric piece that holds up an activistic young pastor as a modern-day Everyman who is counting on his good deeds and his clerical reputation to get him into heaven, whereas the next story, "Philosophy of Life," explores the cost of Christian conviction in terms of marriage and profession, and in contrast with the tendency toward spiritual egotism that can ruin human relationships.

"A Slow, Soft River" by Lawrence Dorr illustrates, through the death of a best friend, the tremendous difficulty of submitting our wills to the will of God — as Jesus did throughout His life, and most notably in the Garden and on the Cross. And the last story in this unit, "Wilbur Finds His Home," is a sympathetic treatment of a forgotten person in our society, a simple old man who is characterized with sensitive insight as a weak and lonely child of God, like all of us, who needs His love and the love and acceptance of other persons.

FLANNERY O'CONNOR

The Artificial Nigger

Mr. Head awakened to discover that the room was full of moonlight. He sat up and stared at the floor boards—the color of silver—and then at the ticking on his pillow, which might have been brocade, and after a second, he saw half of the moon five feet away in his shaving mirror, paused as if it were waiting for his permission to enter. It rolled forward and cast a dignifying light on everything. The straight chair against the wall looked stiff and attentive as if it were awaiting an order and Mr. Head's trousers, hanging to the back of it, had an almost noble air, like the garment some great man had just flung to his servant; but the face on the moon was a grave one. It gazed across the room and out the window where it floated over the horse stall and appeared to contemplate itself with the look of a young man who sees his old age before him.

Mr. Head could have said to it that age was a choice blessing and that only with years does a man enter into that calm understanding of life that makes him a suitable guide for the young. This, at least, had been his own experience.

He sat up and grasped the iron posts at the foot of his bed and raised himself until he could see the face on the alarm clock which sat on an overturned bucket beside the chair. The hour was two in the morning. The alarm on the clock did not work but he was not dependent on any mechanical means to awaken him. Sixty years had not dulled his responses; his physical reactions, like his moral ones, were guided by his will and strong character, and these could be seen plainly in his features. He had a long tube-like face with a long rounded open jaw and a long depressed nose. His eyes were alert but quiet, and in the miraculous moonlight they had a look of composure and of ancient wisdom as if they belonged to one of the great guides of men. He might have been Vergil summoned in the middle of the night to go to Dante, or better, Raphael, awakened by a blast of God's light to fly to the side of Tobias. The only dark spot in the room was Nelson's pallet, underneath the shadow of the window.

Nelson was hunched over on his side, his knees under his chin and his heels under his bottom. His new suit and hat were in the boxes that they had been sent in and these were on the floor at the foot of the pallet where he could get his hands on them as soon as he woke up. The slop jar, out of the shadow and made snow-white in the moonlight, appeared to stand guard over him like a small personal angel. Mr. Head lay back down, feeling entirely confident that he could carry out the moral mission of the coming day. He meant to be up before Nelson and to have the breakfast cooking by the time he awakened. The boy was always irked when Mr. Head was the first up. They would have to leave the house at four to get to the railroad junction by five-thirty. The train was to stop for them at five forty-five and they had to be there on time for this train was stopping merely to accommodate them.

This would be the boy's first trip to the city though he claimed it would be his second because he had been born there. Mr. Head had tried to point out to him that when he was born he didn't have the intelligence to determine his whereabouts but this had made no impression on the child at all and he continued to insist that this was to be his second trip. It would be Mr. Head's third trip. Nelson had said, "I will've already been there twice and I ain't but ten."

Mr. Head had contradicted him.

"If you ain't been there in fifteen years, how you know you'll be able to find your way about?" Nelson had asked. "How you know it hasn't changed some?"

"Have you ever," Mr. Head had asked, "seen me lost?"

Nelson certainly had not but he was a child who was never

satisfied until he had given an impudent answer and he replied, "It's nowhere around here to get lost at."

"The day is going to come," Mr. Head prophesied, "when you'll find you ain't as smart as you think you are." He had been thinking about this trip for several months but it was for the most part in moral terms that he conceived it. It was to be a lesson that the boy would never forget. He was to find out from it that he had no cause for pride merely because he had been born in a city. He was to find out that the city is not a great place. Mr. Head meant him to see everything there is to see in a city so that he would be content to stay at home for the rest of his life. He fell asleep thinking how the boy would at last find out that he was not as smart as he thought he was.

He was awakened at three-thirty by the smell of fatback frying and he leaped off his cot. The pallet was empty and the clothes boxes had been thrown open. He put on his trousers and ran into the other room. The boy had a corn pone on cooking and had fried the meat. He was sitting in the half-dark at the table, drinking cold coffee out of a can. He had on his new suit and his new gray hat pulled low over his eyes. It was too big for him but they had ordered it a size large because they expected his head to grow. He didn't say anything but his entire figure suggested satisfaction at having arisen before Mr. Head.

Mr. Head went to the stove and brought the meat to the table in the skillet. "It's no hurry," he said. "You'll get there soon enough and it's no guarantee you'll like it when you do neither," and he sat down across from the boy whose hat teetered back slowly to reveal a fiercely expressionless face, very much the same shape as the old man's. They were grandfather and grandson but they looked enough alike to be brothers and brothers not too far apart in age, for Mr. Head had a youthful expression by daylight, while the boy's look was ancient, as if he knew everything already and would be pleased to forget it.

Mr. Head had once had a wife and daughter and when the wife died, the daughter ran away and returned after an interval with Nelson. Then one morning, without getting out of bed, she died and left Mr. Head with sole care of the year-old child. He had made the mistake of telling Nelson that he had been born in

Atlanta. If he hadn't told him that, Nelson couldn't have insisted that this was going to be his second trip.

"You may not like it a bit," Mr. Head continued. "It'll be full of niggers."

The boy made a face as if he could handle a nigger.

"All right," Mr. Head said, "you ain't ever seen a nigger."

"You wasn't up very early," Nelson said.

"You ain't ever seen a nigger," Mr. Head repeated. "There hasn't been a nigger in this county since we run that one out twelve years ago and that was before you were born." He looked at the boy as if he were daring him to say he had ever seen a Negro.

"How you know I never saw a nigger when I lived there before?" Nelson asked. "I probably saw a lot of niggers."

"If you seen one you didn't know what he was," Mr. Head said, completely exasperated. "A six-month-old child don't know a nigger from anybody else."

"I reckon I'll know a nigger if I see one," the boy said and got up and straightened his slick sharply creased gray hat and went outside to the privy.

They reached the junction some time before the train was due to arrive and stood about two feet from the first set of tracks. Mr. Head carried a paper sack with some biscuits and a can of sardines in it for their lunch. A coarse-looking orange-colored sun coming up behind the east range of mountains was making the sky a dull red behind them, but in front of them it was still gray and they faced a gray transparent moon, hardly stronger than a thumbprint and completely without light. A small tin switch box and a black fuel tank were all there was to mark the place as a junction; the tracks were double and did not converge again until they were hidden behind the bends at either end of the clearing. Trains passing appeared to emerge from a tunnel of trees and, hit for a second by the cold sky, vanish terrified into the woods again. Mr. Head had had to make special arrangements with the ticket agent to have this train stop and he was secretly afraid it would not, in which case, he knew Nelson would say, "I never thought no train was going to stop for you." Under the useless morning moon the tracks looked white and fragile. Both the old man and the child stared ahead as if they were awaiting an apparition.

Then suddenly, before Mr. Head could make up his mind to turn back, there was a deep warning bleat and the train appeared, gliding very slowly, almost silently around the bend of trees about two hundred yards down the track, with one yellow front light shining. Mr. Head was still not certain it would stop and he felt it would make an even bigger idiot of him if it went by slowly. Both he and Nelson, however, were prepared to ignore the train if it passed them.

The engine charged by, filling their noses with the smell of hot metal and then the second coach came to a stop exactly where they were standing. A conductor with the face of an ancient bloated bulldog was on the step as if he expected them, though he did not look as if it mattered one way or the other to him if they got on or not. "To the right," he said.

Their entry took only a fraction of a second and the train was already speeding on as they entered the quiet car. Most of the travelers were still sleeping, some with their heads hanging off the chair arms, some stretched across two seats, and some sprawled out with their feet in the aisle. Mr. Head saw two unoccupied seats and pushed Nelson toward them. "Get in there by the winder," he said in his normal voice which was very loud at this hour of the morning. "Nobody cares if you sit there because it's nobody in it. Sit right there."

"I heard you," the boy muttered. "It's no use in you yelling," and he sat down and turned his head to the glass. There he saw a pale ghost-like face scowling at him beneath the brim of a pale ghost-like hat. His grandfather, looking quickly too, saw a different ghost, pale but grinning, under a black hat.

Mr. Head sat down and settled himself and took out his ticket and started reading aloud everything that was printed on it. People began to stir. Several woke up and stared at him. "Take off your hat," he said to Nelson and took off his own and put it on his knee. He had a small amount of white hair that had turned tobacco-colored over the years and this lay flat across the back of his head. The front of his head was bald and creased. Nelson took off his hat and put it on his knee and they waited for the conductor to come ask for their tickets.

The man across the aisle from them was spread out over two seats, his feet propped on the window and his head jutting into the aisle. He had on a light blue suit and a yellow shirt unbuttoned at the neck. His eyes had just opened and Mr. Head was ready to introduce himself when the conductor came up from behind and growled, "Tickets."

When the conductor had gone, Mr. Head gave Nelson the return half of his ticket and said, "Now put that in your pocket and don't lose it or you'll have to stay in the city."

"Maybe I will," Nelson said as if this were a reasonable suggestion.

Mr. Head ignored him. "First time this boy has even been on a train," he explained to the man across the aisle, who was sitting up now on the edge of his seat with both feet on the floor.

Nelson jerked his hat on again and turned angrily to the window.

"He's never seen anything before," Mr. Head continued. "Ignorant as the day he was born, but I mean for him to get his fill once and for all."

The boy leaned forward, across his grandfather and toward the stranger. "I was born in the city," he said. "I was born there. This is my second trip." He said it in a high positive voice but the man across the aisle didn't look as if he understood. There were heavy purple circles under his eyes.

Mr. Head reached across the aisle and tapped him on the arm. "The thing to do with a boy," he said sagely, "is to show him all it is to show. Don't hold nothing back."

"Yeah," the man said. He gazed down at his swollen feet and lifted the left one about ten inches from the floor. After a minute he put it down and lifted the other. All through the car people began to get up and move about and yawn and stretch. Separate voices could be heard here and there and then a general hum. Suddenly Mr. Head's serene expression changed. His mouth almost closed and a light, fierce and cautious both, came into his eyes. He was looking down the length of the car. Without turning, he caught Nelson by the arm and pulled him forward. "Look," he said.

A huge coffee-colored man was coming slowly forward. He had on a light suit and a yellow satin tie with a ruby pin in it. One of his hands rested on his stomach which rode majestically under his buttoned coat, and in the other he held the head of a black walking stick that he picked up and set down with a deliberate outward motion each time he took a step. He was proceeding very slowly, his large brown eyes gazing over the heads of the passengers. He had a small white moustache and white crinkly hair. Behind him there were two young women, both coffee-colored, one in a yellow dress and one in a green. Their progress was kept at the rate of his and they chatted in low throaty voices as they followed him.

Mr. Head's grip was tightening insistently on Nelson's arm. As the procession passed them, the light from a sapphire ring on the brown hand that picked up the cane reflected in Mr. Head's eye, but he did not look up nor did the tremendous man look at him. The group proceeded up the rest of the aisle and out of the car. Mr. Head's grip on Nelson's arm loosened. "What was that?" he asked.

"A man," the boy said and gave him an indignant look as if he were tired of having his intelligence insulted.

"What kind of a man?" Mr. Head persisted, his voice expressionless.

"A fat man," Nelson said. He was beginning to feel that he had better be cautious.

"You don't know what kind?" Mr. Head said in a final tone.

"An old man," the boy said and had a sudden foreboding that he was not going to enjoy the day.

"That was a nigger," Mr. Head said and sat back.

Nelson jumped up on the seat and stood looking backward to the end of the car but the Negro had gone.

"I'd of thought you'd know a nigger since you seen so many when you was in the city on your first visit," Mr. Head continued. "That's his first nigger," he said to the man across the aisle.

The boy slid down into the seat. "You said they were black," he said in an angry voice. "You never said they were tan. How do you expect me to know anything when you don't tell me right?"

"You're just ignorant is all," Mr. Head said and he got up and moved over in the vacant seat by the man across the aisle.

Nelson turned backward again and looked where the Negro had disappeared. He felt that the Negro had deliberately walked down the aisle in order to make a fool of him and he hated him with a fierce raw fresh hate and also, he understood now why his grandfather disliked them. He looked toward the window and the face there seemed to suggest that he might be inadequate to the day's exactions. He wondered if he would even recognize the city when they came to it.

After he had told several stories, Mr. Head realized that the man he was talking to was asleep and he got up and suggested to Nelson that they walk over the train and see the parts of it. He particularly wanted the boy to see the toilet so they went first to the men's room and examined the plumbing. Mr. Head demonstrated the ice-water cooler as if he had invented it and showed Nelson the bowl with the single spigot where the travelers brushed their teeth. They went through several cars and came to the diner.

This was the most elegant car in the train. It was painted a rich egg-yellow and had a wine-colored carpet on the floor. There were wide windows over the tables and great spaces of the rolling view were caught in miniature in the sides of the coffee pots and in the glasses. Three very black Negroes in white suits and aprons were running up and down the aisle, swinging trays and bowing and bending over the travelers eating breakfast. One of them rushed up to Mr. Head and Nelson and said, holding up two fingers, "Space for two!" but Mr. Head replied in a loud voice, "We eaten before we left!"

The waiter wore large brown spectacles that increased the size of his eye whites. "Stan' aside then please," he said with an airy wave of the arm as if he were brushing aside flies.

Neither Nelson nor Mr. Head moved a fraction of an inch. "Look," Mr. Head said.

The near corner of the diner, containing two tables, was set off from the rest by a saffron-colored curtain. One table was set but empty but at the other, facing them, his back to the drape, sat the tremendous Negro. He was speaking in a soft voice to the two women while he buttered a muffin. He had a heavy sad face and his neck bulged over his white collar on either side. "They rope them off," Mr. Head explained. Then he said, "Let's go see the kitchen," and they walked the length of the diner but the black waiter was coming fast behind them.

"Passengers are not allowed in the kitchen!" he said in a haughty voice. "Passengers are NOT allowed in the kitchen!"

Mr. Head stopped where he was and turned. "And there's good reason for that," he shouted into the Negro's chest, "because the cockroaches would run the passengers out!"

All the travelers laughed and Mr. Head and Nelson walked out, grinning. Mr. Head was known at home for his quick wit and Nelson felt a sudden keen pride in him. He realized the old man would be his only support in the strange place they were approaching. He would be entirely alone in the world if he were ever lost from his grandfather. A terrible excitement shook him and he wanted to take hold of Mr. Head's coat and hold on like a child.

As they went back to their seats they could see through the passing windows that the countryside was becoming speckled with small houses and shacks and that a highway ran alongside the train. Cars sped by on it, very small and fast. Nelson felt that there was less breath in the air than there had been thirty minutes ago. The man across the aisle had left and there was no one near for Mr. Head to hold a conversation with so he looked out the window, through his own reflection, and read aloud the names of the buildings they were passing. "The Dixie Chemical Corp!" he announced. "Southern Maid Flour! Dixie Doors! Southern Belle Cotton Products! Patty's Peanut Butter! Southern Mammy Cane Syrup!"

"Hush up!" Nelson hissed.

All over the car people were beginning to get up and take their luggage off the overhead racks. Women were putting on their coats and hats. The conductor stuck his head in the car and snarled, "Firstopppppmry," and Nelson lunged out of his sitting position, trembling. Mr. Head pushed him down by the shoulder.

"Keep your seat," he said in dignified tones. "The first stop is on the edge of town. The second stop is at the main railroad station." He had come by this knowledge on his first trip when he had got off at the first stop and had had to pay a man fifteen cents to take him into the heart of town. Nelson sat back down, very pale. For the first time in his life, he understood that his grandfather was indispensable to him.

The train stopped and let off a few passengers and glided on as if it had never ceased moving. Outside, behind rows of brown rickety houses, a line of blue buildings stood up, and beyond them a pale rose-gray sky faded away to nothing. The train moved into the railroad yard. Looking down, Nelson saw lines and lines of silver tracks multiplying and criss-crossing. Then before he could start counting them, the face in the window started out at him, gray but distinct, and he looked the other way. The train was in the station. Both he and Mr. Head jumped up and ran to the door. Neither noticed that they had left the paper sack with the lunch in it on the seat.

They walked stiffly through the small station and came out of a heavy door into the squall of traffic. Crowds were hurrying to work. Nelson didn't know where to look. Mr. Head leaned against the side of the building and glared in front of him.

Finally Nelson said, "Well, how do you see what all it is to see?"

Mr. Head didn't answer. Then as if the sight of people passing had given him the clue, he said, "You walk," and started off down the street. Nelson followed, steadying his hat. So many sights and sounds were flooding in on him that for the first block he hardly knew what he was seeing. At the second corner, Mr. Head turned and looked behind him at the station they had left, a putty-colored terminal with a concrete dome on top. He thought that if he could keep the dome always in sight, he would be able to get back in the afternoon to catch the train again.

As they walked along, Nelson began to distinguish details and take note of the store windows, jammed with every kind of equipment—hardware, drygoods, chicken feed, liquor. They passed one that Mr. Head called his particular attention to where you walked in and sat on a chair with your feet upon two rests and let a Negro polish your shoes. They walked slowly and stopped and stood at the entrances so he could see what went on in each place but they did not go into any of them. Mr. Head was determined not to go into any city store because on his first trip here, he had got lost in a large one and had found his way out only after many people had insulted him.

They came in the middle of the next block to a store that had a weighing machine in front of it and they both in turn stepped up on it and put in a penny and received a ticket. Mr. Head's ticket said, "You weigh 120 pounds. You are upright and brave and all your friends admire you." He put the ticket in his pocket, surprised that the machine should have got his character correct but his weight wrong, for he had weighed on a grain scale not long before and knew he weighed 110. Nelson's ticket said, "You weigh 98 pounds. You have a great destiny ahead of you but beware of dark women." Nelson did not know any women and he weighed only 68 pounds but Mr. Head pointed out that the machine had probably printed the number upside down, meaning the 9 for a 6.

They walked on and at the end of five blocks the dome of the terminal sank out of sight and Mr. Head turned to the left. Nelson could have stood in front of every store window for an hour if there had not been another more interesting one next to it. Suddenly he said, "I was born here!" Mr. Head turned and looked at him with horror. There was a sweaty brightness about his face. "This is where I come from!" he said.

Mr. Head was appalled. He saw the moment had come for drastic action. "Lemme show you one thing you ain't seen yet," he said and took him to the corner where there was a sewer entrance. "Squat down," he said, "and stick you head in there," and he held the back of the boy's coat while he got down and put his head in the sewer. He drew it back quickly, hearing a gurgling in the depths under the sidewalk. Then Mr. Head explained the sewer system, how the entire city was underlined with it, how it contained all the drainage and was full of rats and how a man could slide into it and be sucked along down endless pitchblack tunnels. At any minute any man in the city might be sucked into the sewer and never heard from again. He described it so well that Nelson was for some seconds shaken. He connected the sewer passages with the entrance to hell and understood for the first time how the world was put together in its lower parts. He drew away from the curb.

Then he said, "Yes, but you can stay away from the holes," and his face took on that stubborn look that was so exasperating to his grandfather. "This is where I come from!" he said.

Mr. Head was dismayed but he only muttered, "You'll get your fill," and they walked on. At the end of two more blocks he turned to the left, feeling that he was circling the dome; and he was correct, for in a half-hour they passed in front of the railroad station again. At first Nelson did not notice that he was seeing the same stores twice but when they passed the one where you put your feet on the rests while the Negro polished your shoes, he perceived that they were walking in a circle.

"We done been here!" he shouted. "I don't believe you know where you're at!"

"The direction just slipped my mind for a minute," Mr. Head said and they turned down a different street. He still did not intend to let the dome get too far away and after two blocks in their new direction, he turned to the left. This street contained two- and three-story wooden dwellings. Anyone passing on the sidewalk could see into the rooms and Mr. Head, glancing through one window, saw a woman lying on an iron bed, looking out, with a sheet pulled over her. Her knowing expression shook him. A fierce-looking boy on a bicycle came driving down out of nowhere and he had to jump to the side to keep from being hit. "It's nothing to them if they knock you down," he said. "You better keep closer to me."

They walked on for some time on streets like this before he remembered to turn again. The houses they were passing now were all unpainted and the wood in them looked rotten; the street between was narrower. Nelson saw a colored man. Then another. Then another. "Niggers live in these houses," he observed.

"Well come on and we'll go somewheres else," Mr. Head said. "We didn't come to look at niggers," and they turned down another street but they continued to see Negroes everywhere. Nelson's skin began to prickle and they stepped along at a faster pace in order to leave the neighborhood as soon as possible. There were colored men in their undershirts standing in the doors and colored women rocking on the sagging porches. Colored children played in the gutters and stopped what they were doing to look at them. Before long they began to pass rows of stores with colored customers in them but they didn't pause at the entrances of these. Black eyes in black faces were watching them from every direction. "Yes," Mr. Head said, "this is where you were born — right here with all these niggers."

Nelson scowled. "I think you done got us lost," he said.

Mr. Head swung around sharply and looked for the dome. It was nowhere in sight. "I ain't got us lost either," he said. "You're just tired of walking."

"I ain't tired, I'm hungry," Nelson said. "Give me a biscuit."

They discovered then that they had lost the lunch.

"You were the one holding the sack," Nelson said. "I would have kepaholt of it."

"If you want to direct this trip, I'll go on by myself and leave you right here," Mr. Head said and was pleased to see the boy turn white. However, he realized they were lost and drifting farther every minute from the station. He was hungry himself and beginning to be thirsty and since they had been in the colored neighborhood, they had both begun to sweat. Nelson had on his shoes and he was unaccustomed to them. The concrete sidewalks were very hard. They both wanted to find a place to sit down but this was impossible and they kept on walking, the boy muttering under his breath, "First you lost the sack and then you lost the way," and Mr. Head growling from time to time, "Anybody wants to be from this nigger heaven can be from it!"

By now the sun was well forward in the sky. The odor of dinners cooking drifted out to them. The Negroes were all at their doors to see them pass. "Whyn't you ast one of these niggers the way?" Nelson said. "You got us lost."

"This is where you were born," Mr. Head said. "You can ast one yourself if you want to."

Nelson was afraid of the colored men and he didn't want to be laughed at by the colored children. Up ahead he saw a large colored woman leaning in a doorway that opened onto the sidewalk. Her hair stood straight out from her head for about four inches all around and she was resting on bare brown feet that turned pink at the sides. She had on a pink dress that showed her exact shape. As they came abreast of her, she lazily lifted one hand to her head and her fingers disappeared into her hair.

Nelson stopped. He felt his breath drawn up by the woman's dark eyes. "How do you get back to town?" he said in a voice that did not sound like his own.

After a minute she said, "You in town now," in a rich low tone that made Nelson feel as if a cool spray had been turned on him.

"How do you get back to the train?" he said in the same reed-like voice.

"You can catch you a car," she said.

He understood she was making fun of him but he was too paralyzed even to scowl. He stood drinking in every detail of her. His eyes traveled up from her great knees to her forehead and then made a triangular path from the glistening sweat on her neck down and across her tremendous bosom and over her bare arm back to where her fingers lay hidden in her hair. He suddenly wanted her to reach down and pick him up and draw him against her and then he wanted to feel her breath on his face. He wanted to look down and down into her eyes while she held him tighter and tighter. He had never had such a feeling before. He felt as if he were reeling down through a pitchblack tunnel.

"You can go a block down yonder and catch you a car take you to the railroad station, Sugarpie," she said.

Nelson would have collapsed at her feet if Mr. Head had not pulled him roughly away. "You act like you don't have any sense!" the old man growled.

They hurried down the street and Nelson did not look back at the woman. He pushed his hat sharply forward over his face which was already burning with shame. The sneering ghost he had seen in the train window and all the foreboding feelings he had on the way returned to him and he remembered that his ticket from the scale had said to beware of dark women and that his grandfather's had said he was upright and brave. He took hold of the old man's hand, a sign of dependence that he seldom showed.

They headed down the street toward the car tracks where a long yellow rattling trolley was coming. Mr. Head had never boarded a streetcar and he let that one pass. Nelson was silent. From time to time his mouth trembled slightly but his grandfather, occupied with his own problems, paid him no attention. They stood on the corner and neither looked at the Negroes who were passing, going about their business just as if they had been white, except that most of them stopped and eyed Mr. Head and Nelson. It occured to Mr. Head that since the streetcar ran on tracks, they could simply follow the tracks. He gave Nelson a slight push and explained that they would follow the tracks on into the railroad station, walking, and they set off.

Presently to their great relief they began to see white people again and Nelson sat down on the sidewalk against the wall of a building. "I got to rest myself some," he said. "You lost the sack and the direction. You can just wait on me to rest myself."

"There's the tracks in front of us," Mr. Head said. "All we got to do is keep them in sight and you could have remembered the sack as good as me. This is where you were born. This is your old home town. This is your second trip. You ought to know how to do," and he squatted down and continued in this vein but the boy, easing his burning feet out of his shoes, did not answer.

"And standing there grinning like a chim-pan-zee while a nigger woman gives you direction. Great Gawd!" Mr. Head said.

"I never said I was nothing but born here," the boy said in a shaky voice. "I never said I would or wouldn't like it. I never said I wanted to come. I only said I was born here and I never had nothing to do with that. I want to go home. I never wanted to come in the first place. It was all your big idea. How you know you ain't following the tracks in the wrong direction?"

This last had occurred to Mr. Head too. "All these people are white," he said.

"We ain't passed here before," Nelson said. This was a neighborhood of brick buildings that might have been lived in or might not. A few empty automobiles were parked along the curb and there was an occasional passerby. The heat of the pavement came up through Nelson's thin suit. His eyelids began to droop, and after a few minutes his head tilted forward. His shoulders twitched once or twice and then he fell over on his side and lay sprawled in an exhausted fit of sleep.

Mr. Head watched him silently. He was very tired himself but they could not both sleep at the same time and he could not have slept anyway because he did not know where he was. In a few minutes Nelson would wake up, refreshed by his sleep and very cocky, and would begin complaining that he had lost the sack and the way. You'd have a mighty sorry time if I wasn't here, Mr. Head thought; and then another idea occurred to him. He looked at the sprawled figure for several minutes; presently he stood up. He justified what he was going to do on the grounds that it is sometimes necessary to teach a child a lesson he won't forget, particularly when the child is always reasserting his position with some new impudence. He walked without a sound to the corner about twenty feet away and sat down on a covered garbage can in the alley where he could look out and watch Nelson wake up alone.

The boy was dozing fitfully, half conscious of vague noises and black forms moving up from some dark part of him into the light. His face worked in his sleep and he had pulled his knees up under his chin. The sun shed a dull dry light on the narrow street; everything looked like exactly what it was. After a while Mr. Head, hunched like an old monkey on the garbage can lid, decided that if Nelson didn't wake up soon, he would make a loud noise by bamming his foot against the can. He looked at his watch and discovered that it was two o'clock. Their train left at six and the possibility of missing it was too awful for him to think of. He kicked his foot backwards on the can and a hollow boom reverberated in the alley.

Nelson shot up onto his feet with a shout. He looked where his grandfather should have been and stared. He seemed to whirl several times and then, picking up his feet and throwing his head back, he dashed down the street like a wild maddened pony. Mr. Head jumped off the can and galloped after but the child was almost out of sight. He saw a streak of gray disappearing diagonally a block ahead. He ran as fast as he could, looking both ways down every intersection, but without sight of him again. Then as he passed the third intersection, completely winded, he saw about half a block down the street a scene that stopped him altogether. He crouched behind a trash box to watch and get his bearings.

Nelson was sitting with both legs spread out and by his side lay an elderly woman, screaming. Groceries were scattered about the sidewalk. A crowd of women had already gathered to see justice done and Mr. Head distinctly heard the old woman on the pavement shout, "You've broken my ankle and your daddy'll pay for it! Every nickel! Police!" Several of the women were plucking at Nelson's shoulder but the boy seemed too dazed to get up.

Something forced Mr. Head from behind the trash box and forward, but only at a creeping pace. He had never in his life been accosted by a policeman. The women were milling around Nelson as if they might suddenly all dive on him at once and tear him to pieces, and the old woman continued to scream that her ankle was broken and to call for an officer. Mr. Head came on so slowly that he could have been taking a backward step after each forward one, but when he was about ten feet away, Nelson saw him and sprang. The child caught him around the hips and clung panting against him.

The women all turned on Mr. Head. The injured one sat up and shouted, "You sir! You'll pay every penny of my doctor's bill that your boy has caused. He's a juve-nile delinquent! Where is an officer? Somebody take this man's name and address!"

Mr. Head was trying to detach Nelson's fingers from the flesh in the back of his legs. The old man's head had lowered itself into his collar like a turtle's; his eyes were glazed with fear and caution.

"Your boy has broken my ankle!" the old woman shouted. "Police!"

Mr. Head sensed the approach of the policeman from behind. He stared straight ahead at the women who were massed in their fury like a solid wall to block his escape, "This is not my boy," he said. "I never seen him before."

He felt Nelson's fingers fall out of his flesh.

The women dropped back, staring at him with horror, as if they were so repulsed by a man who would deny his own image and likeness that they could not bear to lay hands on him. Mr. Head walked on, through a space they silently cleared, and left Nelson behind. Ahead of him he saw nothing but a hollow tunnel that had once been the street.

The boy remained standing where he was, his neck craned forward and his hands hanging by his sides. His hat was jammed on his head so that there were no longer any creases in it. The injured woman got up and shook her fist at him and the others gave him pitying looks, but he didn't notice any of them. There was no policeman in sight.

In a minute he began to move mechanically, making no effort to catch up with his grandfather but merely following at about twenty paces. They walked on for five blocks in this way. Mr. Head's shoulders were sagging and his neck hung forward at such an angle that it was not visible from behind. He was afraid to turn his head. Finally he cut a short hopeful glance over his shoulder. Twenty feet behind him, he saw two small eyes piercing into his back like pitchfork prongs.

The boy was not of a forgiving nature but this was the first time he had ever had anything to forgive. Mr. Head had never disgraced himself before. After two more blocks, he turned and called over his shoulder in a high desperately gay voice, "Let's us go get us a Co' Cola somewheres!"

Nelson, with a dignity he had never shown before, turned and stood with his back to his grandfather.

Mr. Head began to feel the depth of his denial. His face as they walked on became all hollows and bare ridges. He saw nothing they were passing but he perceived that they had lost the car tracks. There was no dome to be seen anywhere and the afternoon was advancing. He knew that if dark overtook them in the city, they would be beaten and robbed. The speed of God's justice was only what he expected for himself, but he could not stand to think that his sins would be visited upon Nelson and that even now, he was leading the boy to his doom.

They continued to walk on block after block through an endless section of small brick houses until Mr. Head almost fell over a water spigot sticking up about six inches off the edge of a grass plot. He had not had a drink of water since early morning but he felt he did not deserve it now. Then he thought that Nelson would be thirsty and they would both drink and be brought together. He squatted down and put his mouth to the nozzle and turned a cold stream of water into his throat. Then he called out in the high desperate voice, "Come on and getcher some water!"

This time the child stared through him for nearly sixty seconds. Mr. Head got up and walked on as if he had drunk poison. Nelson, though he had not had water since some he had drunk out of a paper cup on the train, passed by the spigot, disdaining to drink where his grandfather had. When Mr. Head realized this, he lost all hope. His face in the waning afternoon light looked ravaged and abandoned. He could feel the boy's steady hate, traveling at an even pace behind him and he knew that (if by some miracle they escaped being murdered in the city) it would continue just that way for the rest of his life. He knew that now he was wandering into a black strange place where nothing was like it had ever been before, a long old age without respect and an end that would be welcome because it would be the end.

As for Nelson, his mind had frozen around his grandfather's treachery as if he were trying to preserve it intact to present at the final judgment. He walked without looking to one side or the other, but every now and then his mouth would twitch and this was when he felt, from some remote place inside himself, a black mysterious form reach up as if it would melt his frozen vision in one hot grasp.

The sun dropped down behind a row of houses and hardly noticing, they passed into an elegant suburban section where mansions were set back from the road by lawns with birdbaths on them. Here everything was entirely deserted. For blocks they didn't pass even a dog. The big white houses were like partially submerged icebergs in the distance. There were no sidewalks, only drives, and these wound around and around in endless ridiculous circles. Nelson made no move to come nearer to Mr. Head. The old man felt that if he saw a sewer entrance he would drop down into it and let himself be carried away; and he could imagine the boy standing by, watching with only a slight interest, while he disappeared.

A loud bark jarred him to attention and he looked up to see a fat man approaching with two bulldogs. He waved both arms like someone shipwrecked on a desert island. "I'm lost!" he called.

"I'm lost and can't find my way and me and this boy have got to catch this train and I can't find the station. Oh Gawd I'm lost! Oh hep me Gawd I'm lost!"

The man, who was bald-headed and had on golf knickers, asked him what train he was trying to catch and Mr. Head began to get out his tickets, trembling so violently he could hardly hold them. Nelson had come up to within fifteen feet and stood watching.

"Well," the fat man said, giving him back the tickets, "you won't have time to get back to town to make this but you can catch it at the suburb stop. That's three blocks from here," and he began explaining how to get there.

Mr. Head stared as if he were slowly returning from the dead and when the man had finished and gone off with the dogs jumping at his heels, he turned to Nelson and said breathlessly, "We're going to get home!"

The child was standing about ten feet away, his face bloodless under the gray hat. His eyes were triumphantly cold. There was no light in them, no feeling, no interest. He was merely there, a small figure, waiting. Home was nothing to him.

Mr. Head turned slowly. He felt he knew now what time would be like without seasons and what heat would be like without light and what man would be like without salvation. He didn't care if he never made the train and if it had not been for what suddenly caught his attention, like a cry out of the gathering dusk, he might have forgotten there was a station to go to.

He had not walked five hundred yards down the road when he saw, within reach of him, the plaster figure of a Negro sitting bent over on a low yellow brick fence that curved around a wide lawn. The Negro was about Nelson's size and he was pitched forward at an unsteady angle because the putty that held him to the wall had cracked. One of his eyes was entirely white and he held a piece of brown watermelon.

Mr. Head stood looking at him silently until Nelson stopped at a little distance. Then as the two of them stood there, Mr. Head breathed, "An artificial nigger!"

It was not possible to tell if the artificial Negro were meant to be young or old; he looked too miserable to be either. He was meant to look happy because his mouth was stretched up at the corners but the chipped eye and the angle he was cocked at gave him a wild look of misery instead.

"An artificial nigger!" Nelson repeated in Mr. Head's exact tone.

The two of them stood there with their necks forward at almost the same angle and their shoulders curved in almost exactly the same way and their hands trembling identically in their pockets. Mr. Head looked like an ancient child and Nelson like a miniature old man. They stood gazing at the artificial Negro as if they were faced with some great mystery, some monument to another's victory that brought them together in their common defeat. They could both feel it dissolving their differences like an action of mercy. Mr. Head had never known before what mercy felt like because he had been too good to deserve any, but he felt he knew now. He looked at Nelson and understood that he must say something to the child to show that he was still wise and in the look the boy returned he saw a hungry need for that assurance. Nelson's eyes seemed to implore him to explain once and for all the mystery of existence.

Mr. Head opened his lips to make a lofty statement and heard himself say, "They ain't got enough real ones here. They got to have an artificial one."

After a second, the boy nodded with a strange shivering about his mouth, and said, "Let's go home before we get ourselves lost again."

Their train glided into the suburb stop just as they reached the station and they boarded it together, and ten minutes before it was due to arrive at the junction, they went to the door and stood ready to jump off if it did not stop; but it did, just as the moon, restored to its full splendor, sprang from a cloud and flooded the clearing with light. As they stepped off, the sage grass was shivering gently in shades of silver and the clinkers under their feet glittered with a fresh black light. The treetops, fencing the junction like the protecting walls of a garden, were darker than the sky which was hung with gigantic white clouds illuminated like lanterns.

Mr. Head stood very still and felt the action of mercy touch him again but this time he knew that there were no words in the world that could name it. He understood that it grew out of agony, which is not denied to any man and which is given in strange ways to children. He understood it was all a man could carry into death to give his Maker and he suddenly burned with shame that he had so little of it to take with him. He stood appalled, judging himself with the thoroughness of God, while the action of mercy covered his pride like a flame and consumed it. He had never thought himself a great sinner before but he saw now that his true depravity had been hidden from him lest it cause him despair. He realized that he was forgiven for sins from the beginning of time, when he had conceived in his own heart the sin of Adam, until the present, when he had denied poor Nelson. He saw that no sin was too monstrous for him to claim as his own, and since God loved in proportion as He forgave, he felt ready at that instant to enter Paradise.

Nelson, composing his expression under the shadow of his hat brim, watched him with a mixture of fatigue and suspicion, but as the train glided past them and disappeared like a frightened serpent into the woods, even his face lightened and he muttered, "I'm glad I've went once, but I'll never go back again!"

Questions for Reflection and Discussion:

1. Characterize Mr. Head. Does the author deal with him straightforwardly or ironically? What does his name imply?
2. How are "moonlight" and "sunlight" used throughout the story?
3. How does Mr. Head's treatment of blacks demonstrate the way that racial antagonism is frequently taught?
4. Find examples of O'Connor's use of regional dialect, the Southern vernacular.
5. What does the city mean to Mr. Head? To Nelson? How does the *author* use the image of the city in this story?
6. What is the climactic action of the story, and how does O'Connor enhance its significance?

7. Explicate the description of the artificial nigger—do you see any parallels with Christ?
8. How does the artificial nigger relate to the action of mercy defined at the end of the story?
9. What are the deeper implications of "home," "lost," and "station"?

HUGH COOK

Cracked Wheat

...and He to end all strife
The purest wheat in heaven...
Grinds, and kneads up into
this bread of Life.

— Edward Taylor

My first day in Victoria is one of the hottest of the summer. Heat rises from the pavement in sheets so that cars glide toward me in a blur, floating ghostlike above the shimmering street. My tires swish in the melted tar, then pick up pea gravel and throw it against the underside of the van with a clatter. Even away from the inner city there is virtually no breeze. And all of the day's heat seems to find its way into my van, especially the black leather seat which scorches me every time I sit down after a call. The back of my shirt is wet and clings to the leather. Three o'clock, I tell myself. By three o'clock a can of cold pop.

That morning early I caught the first ferry out of Tsawassen to spend a week, my last of the summer, doing Fred Malkoske's bread route. Despite the heat my day goes well, mainly because Fred has given me accurate directions. Most drivers on vacation keep their books up to date, but sometimes the directions are so botched they might as well not be there at all.

I'm not sure just how long it takes Fred to do the route, but judging from the pile of pages left I feel I'm making good time. I guess that's a bit of a thing with me. Each day I try to finish just a bit earlier than the last. That means hustle. Open the back door of the van with the right hand, swing in the metal basket full of bread and pastry with the left, close the door, all in a smooth motion, then run to the front and write down the sale in the book.

I flip the page after another call and the directions read, "Go 2 mi, TR into naval base, 3d on L." I look at the odometer, mentally add two miles and, after passing a road sign that says "Entering Esquimalt," I find the road one tenth of a mile beyond the two. Good old Freddie.

As soon as I make the turn I know I'm right, because all the houses are exactly the same. Not a middle class suburb kind of same, but more a military uniformity, coldly efficient and impersonal, each house with gray stucco at the top and dull blue siding at the bottom. The similarity of the houses in their straight patterned rows reminds me of the precision of a military cemetery.

The women come to the door with baby clutched to hip or with hair curled high around frozen orange juice tins or with portable TV blaring game shows or soap operas from the kitchen counter, all the women numbly taking their white sliced and then retreating into the anonymity of their identical houses.

One breaks the pattern.

The route book says cracked wheat—one of the few I sell. I walk up the steps off the driveway and knock on the screen door, thinking that anybody who eats cracked wheat can't be all bad.

A woman opens and says, "Oh yes, let me get the money."

I watch her through the screen door but my eyes are used to the bright sunlight, so that the kitchen is nothing but a green haze and I can't quite make her out as she rummages through her purse. I see only a pair of white, sharply creased slacks. They come to the door.

"Can you change a five?" she asks.

I open the screen door, wedge the basket between my hip and the doorpost, and reach into my pocket for the change.

"I'll tell you what," she says, "why don't you step in out of the sun. That way the flies don't come in either." I do as she says and then she looks at me. "My but you look hot. And no wonder. It's supposed to get up to 94 today."

"Yeah, it's pretty mean out there. Feels nice and cool in here, though." My neck is feeling chafed where the sweat drips into the irritation caused by my shaving.

"Would you like a cold drink?" she asks me.

She's an angel, and I can't resist. "If it isn't too much trouble."

"Not at all. Why don't you sit down a moment." She doesn't ask me but says it, as if there's no question.

She clunks two ice cubes into a tall glass, pours in some Coke and hands it to me, the pop fizzing in the ice. Then she sits down on a red stool by the kitchen counter, feet resting on one of the rungs, shoulders hunched slightly forward like a little bird. She lights a cigarette and I watch her. Her hair is red, hanging loose to her shoulders, the sides swept forward, nicely to two points. The fingers holding the cigarette by her chin are long and thin; the other hand lies palm up on her knee, the blue veins at her wrist standing out like strings pulled taut between elbow and hand.

"Are you a relief driver with the bakery?" she asks.

"Yes, I do this just during the summers. I'm a student."

Usually people are content to leave it at that, but she asks me whether I go to UVic here.

No, I tell her, I live in Vancouver, which is an honest answer but also, I realize immediately, an evasive one.

She persists. "You go where then, UBC?"

At that point I realize I'll have to explain. I tell her that I attend a church-related college in the States and that I plan to enter the ministry.

I'm not sure what she'll say to that, if her reaction to religion is as hesitant as most people's. But she startles me completely by saying, "Well, delivery man or minister, either way you give people bread, right?"

Now, I had not thought of that before—as a matter of fact, the last two summers I'd begun to feel almost as if I were living in two worlds which hardly seemed to touch each other; nine months I live as a student in a world abstract, systematic, and therefore governable; my summers at work, however, are concrete and often chaotic, so removed from a sense of purpose that they've become a means rather than an end, which violates the teaching of my upbringing that *all* of life is holy vocation—and therefore, once I get beyond the ingenuity of her metaphor I realize that there is a deeper truth there that instantly bridges my two seemingly alien worlds.

I guess the shock recognition of it must have shown on my face, for she says with a trace of amused complicity, "We're Catholic. Not very good ones, but still Catholic."

But I'm feeling only the shame of realizing suddenly that my practice has been inconsistent with my confession, and I guess the rest of what I'm recounting here demonstrates how difficult it is to evict the contradictions that lodge stubbornly as squatters in our lives.

The bakery route is divided into two runs, a M-W-F one and a T-Th. The next day, all goes well on the T-Th run. It's the shorter of the two, and I finish at five o'clock.

Wednesday morning I load beside Kenny Greene. "How's it goin' on Freddie's route?" he asks me.

"Oh, not bad. No problem so far."

The sky is clear and a cool morning breeze blows in off the water of the harbour. Later it will be hot again.

"You managin' to get rid of the load OK?"

"I had a bit left over yesterday, I think because of the heat. Too many people out. But I should be able to get rid of it at a freezer call today, so things are going pretty well. No sweat."

"Just make sure so's none a the customers runs up their bill yea high. I been at this goin' twenty years, and you gotta watch summa them. They'll skip out on ya and leave ya holdin' a bill for fifteen lousy bucks."

"I'm watching it pretty well," I tell him. What does he think I am, a rookie?

Then he looks at me. "You got a girl back home? Must be tough durin' the week, huh?" He looks at me out of the corner of his eye and laughs.

"I don't have a girlfriend, actually."

"Aw c'mon, a young fella like you? Don't gimme any a that. Besides, who needs a girlfriend? I know what's happenin' at the universities. I wasn't born yesterday, you know," and he guffaws.

I laugh, letting him interpret it any way he wants.

The day turns out hot, so hot that the van feels as if it should be baking the bread, not just carrying it. But I make good time, and am ahead of schedule when I reach Mrs. Borelli, my cracked wheat lady.

"The usual," she says to me from inside. I wait on the porch, then she opens the screen door, takes the bread, and gives me the exact change.

"You look like you could use a repeat on that cold drink," she tells me, and stands aside holding the screen door open so I can carry my basket through.

I hesitate. It's not often people invite me in, and I hate to finish late. But I know her kitchen is cool, and a cold drink sounds good, so I step inside, placing my basket on the red-tiled floor gently so as not to scratch the wax finish.

She pulls back a chair for me, goes to the refrigerator, takes a glass out of the top freezer, and pours in the drink. When she brings the glass to me it's covered with a glaze of frost, and I'm moved by her thoughtfulness. She had it ready for me.

"How did you know to take cracked wheat to the door the first day?" she asks me.

Somehow she has made me feel loose and I tell her, "The moment I saw your house I said to myself this looks like a cracked wheat kind of place," but as soon as I say it I remember the similarity of the houses in the base, and I'm not sure whether this makes my attempt at a joke even funnier or totally absurd. With panic I think the latter.

But she laughs. She sits down on the stool, her red hair swept back this time over her ears and gathered at the back, like she might be an artist. Her face is deeply tanned and she looks cool.

"You must be almost done for the summer, I guess."

"As a matter of fact, this is my last week. Monday I head back to school."

"And you haven't even told me your name," she says, feigning offense.

"Oh yeah. Neil Van Wyk." She has a habit of speaking rapidly, and I find myself speeding up my own words, carried along in her momentum like a car caught in the draught of a large truck.

"Van Wyk — is that Dutch?"

"Uh huh. My parents immigrated in '52 when I was four."

"I guess you don't remember much of Holland then."

"Not really."

She drops her chin then and smiles, as if to tease me. "Supposed to be hard-working people, the Dutch."

"No more than anybody else, I suppose. But they do have a mania about keeping things clean. You should see my mother — she even scrubs the driveway!"

We both laugh. I'm surprised to find myself conversing with this woman as an equal. In high school the girls had always seemed so sure of themselves, so carefree, while I was always reticent, aware of being Dutch, and I was afraid that made me different. But with her I'm feeling at ease.

"How about you — you must be Italian, with a name like Borelli."

"I'm not, but my husband is."

Then it's my turn to tease. "I didn't think Italians had red hair."

"But with a woman you never know, do you?" she says point blank, and immediately I feel her superiority and I don't know what to say just then. I look around self-consciously. Children's art work covers one of the glossy red kitchen walls. There is a paper mosaic of a sailor in white bellbottoms, the hands large where the child had difficulty cutting the pieces small enough. Beneath the sailor in a child's scrawl is the word "daddy." Beside it, a sheet of red paper shows Humpty-Dumpty sitting on a brick wall, the oval shape made of little pieces of egg shell glued to the paper.

"Your kids'?"

"Yes, the children did those. Hanging things up, I find, encourages them. The egg thing was done by Danny, who's eight, and the others are Gina's. She's ten. They did them at the park. They have a really fine summer arts and crafts program there, and the kids just love it. What with it and the swimming pool, they spend all afternoon there, and I mean all afternoon. I don't know whether to enjoy the peace and quiet, or hate the loneliness."

She lights a cigarette, blows the smoke out slowly through

pursed lips, and seems suddenly pensive, as if she's all by herself. Then she says, "Have you ever wished you could be a child again? Seriously—just be able to do it all over again?"

I'm not sure I have ever felt that.

"I sometimes wish that," she says. Her eyes turn away from me and narrow, as if her eyes are bad and she's trying to focus on an object in the distance. "But then again, maybe things wouldn't be all that different. Because you wouldn't know then what you do now, would you?"

I tell her I suppose not.

"It sure would be nice, though," she muses.

"What would you do different?" I ask her. It's hard for me to imagine my own life being much different from what it has been, as if past events have both an unquestioned inevitability and place.

"Well, I would study, like you. I had always intended to—Well, I wouldn't have gotten married so soon, for another."

"Would you really?"

"Yes, I was crazy!" Her voice turns husky in self-reproof. "Romantic fool that I was, falling in love with a sailor's uniform. And me only nineteen."

Only nineteen. I'm wondering how old she thinks *I* am.

"I look at the children now," she continues, "and I remember what it was like, how we trusted everything and everyone. It was easier to believe, somehow, back then. In yourself, other people, the church—do you know what I mean? You just didn't doubt that things could be any different from the way they were—or that they should be. Everything fit. When your parents said something, you trusted them. Same with the church. Somehow, when the priest spoke, you were certain, and when you felt the host on your tongue—oh, I had visions of the broken body!"

Her eyes stare wide at nothing in particular as she speaks, her impassioned tone surprising me. And I don't know just what to say to her, feel totally incapable of forming any words, even though I want to, and to leave seems at the moment such a temptation.

"Listen, I just *have* to run. I've a couple of hours to go yet, and it's way past three." It's an awkward moment in the conversation to leave, and my clumsiness shows it.

But her embarrassment is equal to mine. "I'm sorry, I didn't mean to detain you."

"That's all right. I forgot about the time. I'll see you Friday."

I step out, carefully closing the screen door so the spring will not make it slam.

I finish the route later than before.

"They didn't give me my two lousy pumpernickel," Kenny Greene complains to me Friday morning as we load our trucks. "They never give me what I order. So what am I supposed to tell the customer. Huh? You tell me."

"Yeah, bad news."

"Them cruds — hey! Last day on the Island, right? I almost forgot. So, poor Freddie's comin' back to the grind on Monday. Well, every party's got to end sometime. Right?"

"I suppose."

I continue loading my van. White sliced on the left, where I can reach them easily; beside them the brown sliced, then the assorted: whole wheat, sesame seed, buttertop, and unsliced fancy.

I want to get an early start. My last day. Of all days to catch the early ferry, this is the one. But I'll have to make good time — and not have too many tourists at the ferry slip in Schwartz Bay.

Kenny breaks my daydream. "Weekend comin' up, eh? Some fast action, I bet. Yeah, I guess!"

I try to ignore him.

"Hey, the Mainland girls·any better than the Island ones you saw? Huh? You shouldn't leave so quick. You're not gettin' a taste of the local talent." Then he's close to me, nudging me in the ribs with his elbow. "Well, it's probably just as well you're leavin', cuz all those lonely babes in the naval base'll be havin' the hots for ya purty soon. Yeah, waddya expect, with all the hubbies havin' a good time over there in the Mediterranean and them places. You didn't know that, didja. Smart university kid!"

I finish loading and swing shut the doors of the van. "See ya, Kenny. Take care."

"Yeah, be good. Hey, and take it easy on the ladies!"

The route goes smoothly. The weather is hot, but not uncomfortable. I arrive at Mrs. Borelli's house much earlier than usual, and she is surprised to see me.

"Oh, you've caught me early," she says. "I must look a fright." She runs a comb through her hair and brushes her slacks nervously with her hand. Then she says for me to sit.

I feel slightly on edge. My intention was not to stay—at least, not for long, because I'm feeling on the verge of having completed my summer, and if I can only finish it now, the little bit left, I'll be done. But I'm feeling too that I've enjoyed talking with her, and I know that she intends for me to stay a bit, and that she'll be disappointed if I don't.

"Well, your last day," she says, placing the cold drink on the table in front of me. "It's a special occasion, and I've got a little something for you. I was going to wrap it, but you came too early." She walks to the counter, then says, "Close your eyes now, and don't open them until I say."

I close my eyes. I haven't expected this, whatever it is.

"This is for you," she says, holding out a book. Hardbound. Something about the meaning of faith. "I hope you like it."

I'm riffling through the pages, shaking my head.

"I know, I shouldn't have done it, right? Wrong. I want you to have it."

She sits down on the stool, not at the counter now, but with me at the table. She doesn't seem nervous anymore. I smell her perfume, aware of it for the first time.

"I—that's very good of you."

She doesn't say anything, content for the moment to watch me and enjoy my surprise at her gift. I'm thinking of something to say, trying to break the silence.

"I guess your husband sees quite a bit of the world."

"Yes, I suppose he does." She forces a smile.

"Where's he stationed now?"

"In Cyprus."

I feel awkward about the conversation, but it feels almost as if it's steering itself and all I can do is plunge on.

"When will he be home?"

"October."

"Phew."

"Yes, I know," she concedes.

"What do you do, have a part-time job? I mean, how do you manage to fill the time?"

Her lip curls in a rueful smile. "Well, you learn to do a lot on your own. And don't forget, there's the kids. They permit you to do only so much. But otherwise? Well, I read a fair bit, make some of my own clothes. . . . It's funny though—do you know how many social things assume you come in couples? And if you don't, you don't fit. Even at the parish. What I get there is sympathy, and that I don't need. You don't break loneliness with sympathy. You can't invite it over for a cup of coffee."

At that moment I sense how different her life is from my own, and how hard it is for me to meet hers. Besides, what can I do in my last visit, such a brief moment. Behind her on the wall the second hand of the clock glides in a smooth, inexorable arc, and to go seems so inviting, to glide as smooth as the second hand, and I rise slowly.

"It's getting on and I want to thank you very much—" but she places her hand lightly on my arm, urging me back to my seat.

"Are you always this way?" She laughs.

"What—you mean—"

"Rushing off. Relax! Time goes fast enough without you pushing it."

I tell her no really, I should go, and that I'm grateful—and then her expression softens and she looks suddenly fragile and thin. Then she rises slowly from her stool, head down, comes close to me and grasps my elbows, and then she raises her head to look at me. I'm surprised to see that her eyes are suddenly wet and staring into mine with a desperation I have never seen before as they plead Don't leave me. Then she draws me to herself and her hands hold my back and I hold her, close my eyes, and smooth her hair with my hand, her lips kissing my neck—and suddenly I see Kenny Greene's leering face and I jerk back my arms in shock.

The woman slumps down on the stool, hair over her face, weeping, and I feel I can't leave like this, not without her letting me go, and I walk to her stool and touch her shoulder. She doesn't move, and then I'm torn about what to do.

I run out. The screen door snaps shut behind me, and when I hear the clap I wince, as if the broken hand of Christ Himself has slapped me in the face.

Questions for Reflection and Discussion:

1. Why do you think that the author used first-person narration in this story? Why the present tense?
2. What words and phrases in the description immediately incline the reader to sympathize with the young wife?
3. How do "white sliced" and "cracked wheat" contrast in the story?
4. Explain the significance of the juxtaposition of the sailor and the Humpty-Dumpty (children's art work) on the kitchen wall.
5. How does Mrs. Borelli remind Neil that the Christian life is unified?
6. What role does Kenny play in Neil's development during the summer?
7. What stereotypes in the mind of this young Protestant are shattered when Mrs. Borelli reflects on her faith?
8. What is Mrs. Borelli's main problem?
9. What deeper meaning does "cracked wheat" have in the light of the epigraph from Edward Taylor and of the concluding sentence of the story?
10. Why does the young man feel as he does when he leaves Mrs. Borelli at the end of the story?

WALTER LOCKWOOD

A Compassion Man

Reverend Peter Carpenter limped smiling into Mrs. Dunlap's
living room, not noticing till he sat on the crushed velvet ottoman that his shoe was rapidly filling with blood. One of the
dozen parishioners who comprised the week's book club took a
moment to point out the spreading stain on his left sock.

"I guess she got through to the flesh after all," he laughed, lifting the foot for Mrs. Dunlap to see. She sedately pressed a silver-
encrusted cameo, measuring the situaiton. The old flesh shud-
dered just a bit; no one noticed but him, he was sure. A bloody
foot certainly would not do on a white wool carpet.

"Come, Reverend Peter. Mrs. Howard will patch you up in the
kitchen. I'm so sorry, my dear. Renée has been terribly nervous
since the neighbor boy took up riding a motorcycle. It makes a
frightful noise. Poor puppy. She's been biting everything lately.
Shall I run you up for a tetanus shot?"

"I'm sure Renée is less apt to be rabid than I am, Lucille."

An appreciative burst of laughter set his palms burning and
perspiring in the odd way they did whenever he was pleasantly
embarrassed.

Mrs. Howard, a stout black woman with red processed hair,
swayed to some silent tune as she ironed Mr. Dunlap's under-
shorts. Mrs. Dunlap motioned her with a pale, veiny finger.

"Mrs. Howard, Reverend Peter has cut his heel. Please get the
first-aid kit and patch him up."

Mrs. Howard looked up slowly. "Yes'm," she said, languidly

placing the iron on end, folding the shorts, setting them in a plastic basket.

"Quickly, please! The group is waiting."

She nodded, shuffling slowly toward the bathroom. She wore old corduroy bedroom slippers from which stuck two legs like enormous smoked Virginia hams.

When she had disappeared down the vaulted hallway, past the corner where the marble Hebe stood in her arched recess, he spoke.

"Her legs. What does she have?"

"Elephantiasis, or some terrible thing. Poor creature. She's getting so indolent I may have to let her go. Please sit, Peter. Get off that foot." She gently persuaded him onto the stool the cleaning woman had left. "Your sermon today was very good. Not so intellectual as some of the other ones. You must quote poetry more slowly, dear. I think I know you well enough to tell you that."

Peter hid the pain of this brief, irritating gouge by bending to remove his shoe. "I'll remember that, Lucille. I'm still learning, of course."

"You certainly are. And doing. The church was never so active before you arrived."

Again he felt the heat in his hands as he peeled back the bloody sock. "I am a servant. I'm not afraid to get my hands dirty."

She placed a hand on his shoulder. The veins were large, snaky, the color and texture of nightcrawlers. "Some of us think it is unfortunate that you are only the assistant minister, Peter."

"That's kind of you, Lucille. But I have great respect for Dr. Boatwright."

"Of course you do. We all have. But you are so ambitious. Such a breath of fresh air. Dr. Boatwright would have never considered inviting colored—but I'll tell you later. Mrs. Howard, here you are at last. You see Reverend Peter hasn't yet bled to death."

"Yes'm," the woman said, straining to drop to her knees.

"No, no. You mustn't do that. I can tape it myself. Please get up, Mrs. Howard."

Mrs. Dunlap waved a hand at him. "Mrs. Howard *wants* to do it, Peter. Don't you, Mrs. Howard?"

"Yes'm, I do."

Peter shrugged weakly, embarrassed at the huge woman kneeling at his feet. As she cleaned the puncture with cotton and alcohol, he watched her hands. They were swift and nimble as a physician's, completely unlike the rest of her. He found himself feeling very fond of Mrs. Howard, though she had not spoken a word to him.

"Mrs. Howard," he said. "Your legs. What is your condition?"

Without looking away from the bandage she was preparing, she answered, "Doctor said it was my glands."

"Has he prescribed anything for you?"

"Yes, sir. But that was a long time ago. I ain't seen him lately."

"Was he too expensive?"

"Yes, sir."

"Lucille, get me paper and a pencil. Mrs. Howard, I'm going to give you the address of the free clinic I've organized. You come in tomorrow. Today, if you wish. We have doctors, nurses, the whole business. Please come. I want to help you out."

"Yes, sir, I'll come." She raised her head a moment and held him with her weary eyes. He scribbled the address of the clinic and slipped the note into her apron pocket.

"Good! Now if there's anything else I can help you with, let me know. Do you have a family?"

"Five children, Reverend. My husband is dead."

"I'm sorry. Please, Mrs. Howard. If your family needs clothing . . . anything, just contact me. We—"

"Reverend *Peter*." Mrs. Dunlap's smile had frozen. She touched his elbow with a sharp, peach fingernail. "The group, Peter. We mustn't keep them waiting."

"Yes, of course. Thank you, Mrs. Howard, for ministering to me. You have very gentle hands."

Mrs. Dunlap took his arm and led him into the dining room. She paused a moment amid the gleam of silver teapots and saucers and delicate spoons. Cakes and breads, like small clusters of flowers, covered her silver platters.

"Peter," she whispered. "You must promise not to tell Mrs.

Howard about the church's Second-Best Store. It would mortify me if my maid were seen buying our hand-me-downs. Do you understand?"

Peter looked at her, managing a stiff smile. Mollify, he thought. It is the necessary evil of the profession.

"Of course, Lucille. I won't mention it unless she asks."

"Ah, Peter. You understand us, my dear. You are a most amenable man."

As Peter resumed his seat on the ottoman, he was momentarily disarmed by the thought that something important had been overlooked. The retreat banquet followed this meeting, and the anti-war panel at nine. This was Sunday. Wasn't there something else on Sunday? Before he could reconstruct his schedule, Mrs. Dunlap suggested that they begin the meeting with a prayer.

"Fine, Lucille. I have one handy. I don't recall having prayed in one shoe before, but I'll give it a turn."

As he spoke words of thanks, he noticed that Henry Piper had worn white loafers and white socks. He was glad of this casual note. He had worn a turtle neck specifically to put them at ease, to create a more relaxed, seminar atmosphere. They had all worn ties. Apparently, though, no one was bothered by his informality.

Mrs. Dunlap introduced a little lady, a Mrs. Much, as her neighbor and a devout Catholic. Peter nodded to the tiny creature, she politely returning the gesture, upsetting a cluster of wooden grapes stapled to the brim of an enormous floppy hat.

"I haven't read the book," she said. "I'm here to listen to what you Presbyterians have to say."

"I haven't read it either, dear," Mrs. Dunlap said. "I tried once but it bored me. I was hoping to sit back tonight myself and listen to the gentlemen."

Henry Piper, the city's foremost appliance dealer, yawned and stretched his legs, brushed some dandruff from his orange sport coat and said, "I skimmed some of it, but those Winesburg weirdos got irritating after a while."

"I got through half of it," Dr. Goodrich, the urologist, said, folding one leg neatly over the other. "But I'll have something to say, naturally."

The others laughed, knowing Dr. Goodrich's outspokenness on

all matters, medical or otherwise. Peter felt a momentary panic. He had scheduled a two hour meeting, and only fifteen minutes had passed.

Henry Piper, known as something of a jester, said, "You want to try another prayer, Reverend Pete?"

Peter smiled. "Well, I hope *someone* has read it."

"We have," the Tolivers said together. Finn Toliver was a third grade teacher with a wispy, half-hearted beard and an enormously pregnant wife.

"Good. Who else?"

The others reluctantly admitted their feeble efforts. There hadn't been enough time, they said. Spring was a busy season.

"All right, then, we'll do our best. Let's begin by defining what Anderson meant by the term 'grotesque.' Who are they and what—"

"Hold on a minute, Reverend Peter." It was Dr. Goodrich, leaning forward, elbows on his knees. "I hope you don't mean to assault us with a lot of Freudian nonsense again. Let's just look at the book."

"I could, but I won't, Dr. Goodrich. This time I promise."

"Good." Henry Piper leaned back in Mrs. Dunlap's bentwood rocker. Peter prepared himself. "You fellows that put all those symbols in books. Why, a common fellow like me gets to thinking you're just symbol minded."

Henry guffawed and Dr. Goodrich slapped his back. Mrs. Dunlap nodded approvingly.

Finn Toliver's wife, who apparently felt herself one of the fellows Henry was speaking of, said, "Listen, Henry, symbols do exist, you know. They *do* exist."

"That's right, Henry." Finn quickly picked up the ball, interrupting something his wife was about to say. "Symbols are a perfectly legitimate literary device—"

"And if they're *revelant,* we should talk about them," his wife said. "Anything that's *revelant* we should talk about."

Peter felt himself redden, wondering if he should take the initiative and correct her. He looked at Finn, now silent, chewing the knuckle of his forefinger. Peter decided against it.

"These people are all desperately alone," he said, answering his original question. "They are grotesque because they can't express what they really are. They were once all lovers, dreamers, beautiful human beings. But somewhere along the line their humanity has been outraged and they have settled in Winesburg to hide from that pain. Each story shows the desperate attempt of each of them to reach out to someone else—usually to George Willard, the young main character. But they all fail. They get scared and withdraw from that commitment. As readers we get to see the beauty of these odd people, these outcasts. Anderson calls upon us to exercise understanding and compassion. To look about us, find such people, and reach out to them."

"That's very good," Finn Toliver said. "I didn't see that."

"Yes you did, honey. We discussed it at home."

"I mean I didn't see it *that clearly.*"

"I didn't see it that way at all." It was Henry Piper, pulling at a Dutch Master, serious now. "I got sick of them. I mean it! They're a bunch of flops as far as I'm concerned. Even George Willard. When his old man told him to stop dreaming and acting like a gawky girl, that appealed to me. None of them had any get up and go. I wouldn't hire a single one, George included."

Dr. Goodrich grinned at his friend's candor. "Settle down, Henry. Not everybody is cut out for the appliance business."

"Well, more of them should be. They'd get along better."

Peter smiled and pointed, catching Henry's attention. "You, Henry, are a self-made man. I can understand your irritation at people who can't lift themselves out of the holes they've dug. But these people are all around us. They need a hand—a strong hand like yours. I think that's what Anderson was trying to say. Christ said much the same thing."

Henry quickly nodded, finding Jesus more agreeable than Anderson. Peter sensed he had struck a note no one could find dissonant. He resolved to pursue it.

"Not to change the subject," Dr. Goodrich interrupted, "but Finn here says the doctor in that fourth story performed an abortion on his girlfriend, and she died as a result. I say that's pure poppycock. It's medically unsound."

Finn redddened, leaning away from his wife. "Well, I'm no doctor."

"You sure aren't," Dr. Goodrich said, grinning.

"Let's talk about it," Peter said. "I'm inclined to agree with Finn."

"Let's talk about that window-peeping Presbyterian minister. That one I liked," Henry Piper said, winking at Peter.

"It sounds like something you'd pick." Dr. Goodrich nodded wisely.

Finn stroked his corn silk beard, ignoring the jocularity. "The story 'Godliness' was my personal favorite. All of you may disagree, but I feel it points out very strongly the corruptive power of wealth, even on a religious man."

There was a moment of heavy silence. Peter's eye strayed to the gossamer window and the bevy of Cadillacs parked at the curb. Finn's Rambler was a leper in their midst.

The glance outside awakened in him the same rankling of something undone, something overlooked. *What was it?* He swiftly pushed into the haze of memory, but ceased when he realized the silence was growing unbearable. They were all waiting for him.

"I would agree with your conclusion, Finn," he said quickly. "Though I don't think Anderson means to generalize beyond this specific case. Christ did not oppose wealth honestly earned and unselfishly possessed. He was no ascetic, you know. Christ believed in richness of life, not suppression of it. 'By thy fruits shall ye be known.' Why do you think he said that John the Baptist was first on earth, but the least in heaven was greater than he? I think he meant that John, the holy ascetic, the man who turned the hair of his shirt inward against his flesh, had not truly learned the beauty of a full and fruitful life."

"Amen," Dr. Goodrich said, straightening his bright silk tie.

"That was very well put, Peter," Mrs. Dunlap said. "My husband, Mr. Dunlap, has worked hard for what we have. And I believe he has been more than generous with his substance."

Peter scented danger in the direction of the conversation, but a response was unavoidable. "He certainly has, Lucille. All of you have."

"You bet!" Henry Piper spoke through his steaming Dutch Master. "I give a pile to the church so it can help poor slobs like this Winesburg bunch. I don't mind it. It makes me feel good. Otherwise I wouldn't do it."

"I didn't mean to point a finger," Finn said quietly.

"Oh, we know that, Finn." Peter briskly patted Finn's knee. "Listen, we'd better get into at least one of these stories before Mrs. Howard has the coffee out."

"I want you to show me where you see an abortion anywhere in this book . . ." And with that, Dr. Goodrich began a long philippic. Before he had finished, Peter noticed that Mrs. Much, dear lady, was fast asleep.

Three coffees and a half dozen ginger cakes later, Peter stood at Mrs. Dunlap's door, shaking hands all around and touching the ladies' shoulders. Through a corner of his eye he noticed Renée safely roped now to a crabapple tree. Mrs. Howard had washed the blood from his sock, and he'd borrowed a pair of Mr. Dunlap's to wear to the banquet.

Mrs. Dunlap, acting the gracious hostess, moved beside him and took his arm. "Your dear Eleanor must be a very understanding wife, Peter. You are always on the go. Your pace would wear me to a frazzle."

"She's the strength behind me, Lucille. I'd never manage without her. She knows the demands of my job."

"You're a lucky young man."

"And a very wise one," Mrs. Much said, grasping his hand. "You know, Reverend Carpenter, something you said struck me deeply. It was when you were speaking of George Willard's mother dying and George beginning to look backwards for the first time in his life. Do you remember?"

"Certainly I do."

"Well, do you know that I never really looked backwards until this year. You see, all of my friends have begun dying. I'm seventy-one."

"George is morbid," Henry Piper said. "Living in the past at eighteen. It's sick."

"I don't think —" Peter began.

"I mean, why didn't I begin looking backwards sooner?"

Peter sighed silently and loosened his grip on Mrs. Much's hand. "It is because you are strong in faith, Mrs. Much. George hadn't found the answers that you obviously have."

"Of course," she said gleefully. "That must be it. Lucille, this young man should have been a priest."

"I'm sorry, Emily dear. He's ours and we're keeping him."

Henry Piper came close and firmly gripped Peter's biceps. "By heavens, Peter, I wish I had you in the appliance business. Not many have the spunk you do."

Peter laughed. "I'm afraid I wouldn't make much of a salesman, Henry."

"Nonsense. You sell, Peter. You sell compassion, boy. That's the toughest product on the market. I'm an appliance man; you're a compassion man."

Peter laughed again, but was disconcerted to find that Henry was perfectly serious.

"Well, Lucille, all of you. I really must be going. The retreat banquet begins in half an hour. Our seniors are waiting for me at the church. So—" he raised his arms—"let us pray. Dear God, give us wisdom to perceive the truths of this fine book, strength to carry out its message of human communion, courage to touch one another and open our hearts, and compassion to reach out and help those who cannot help themselves. We ask all this in the name of your son, Jesus Christ, God and Savior of all mankind. Amen."

And out the door he flew, down through an archway of flaming wisteria. He set the frantic, screaming poodle reeling in his wake.

It was midnight before Reverend Carpenter returned to the church for his car. His belly was still heavy from the banquet and the half dozen coffees he'd consumed since the book club, so he decided to leave the car and walk it off. As he approached the kitchen door to drop the keys inside, he was surprised to find a light in Dr. Boatwright's office. The door was unlocked, so he went in, startling the old man writing busily at his desk.

"Still up?"

"Oh, hello, Peter. You gave me a flutter. Say, Eleanor has called several times tonight."

"I had the anti-war panel at First Methodist, Walter. Wepman got hot and nearly wrecked the spirit of the thing. Par for the course. It was well attended, though. A lot of blacks and young people."

Dr. Boatwright had a loose, orbicular face that was trained to quiver with his oratory. In the dim light his flesh looked very grey. "She said her parents were over. They expected you home."

"Oh, good grief, I guess I forgot to mention the panel to her. How did she sound?"

"Mildly irritated."

"Oh, boy."

"You should take it easy, Peter. Believe me, there's just so much Peter Carpenter to go around."

Peter laughed and dropped the keys on his desk. "You can't keep a man from laboring in the vineyards, can you? Here, keep my keys. I've got to walk off a couple pounds of fried chicken. Just look at this gut! I'm being banqueted to death. I'll be portly by thirty-five."

Dr. Boatwright smiled. "Think about what I said, Peter. Take it easy. And good luck with Eleanor."

"Thanks, Walter. I won't see you till Saturday. Eleanor can pick up the car. I'll be up at camp for senior retreat tomorrow."

"Ah, that's right. I hope you can get through to those young people. I'm afraid they're nearly beyond me. Goodnight, Peter."

"Don't worry, Walter. I feel for them. Their problems are real. I take the time to listen. Be good now. Goodnight."

Before Peter had gone three blocks he began to wish he'd driven home. He wondered why in the world Eleanor's parents had come into town. Why hadn't she mentioned it? She was always making plans without concern for his schedule. No doubt there would be righteous indignation to face again this night. His stomach tightened; the fried chicken became a pile of rocks. As he walked a ghostly row of poplars, his side began to ache. The moon appeared from under flying clouds, and Ellis's hound howled gloomily.

At last he approached his back door and quietly entered the kitchen. As he reached to switch on the light above the sink, something gouged his finger; he cried out sharply. When the light was on, he saw that his wife had left dishes draining in the sink. A paring knife, blade upward, had pierced his forefinger.

"Well done, Eleanor," he muttered, sucking his wound.

At the basement door he heard the pathetic cries of her Siamese cat. She hadn't even bothered to feed the blasted thing. As he bandaged his finger, his irritation grew. He's never disliked a cat as he did this one. It whined like a spoiled child and bothered him till it got what it wanted. Well, it would wait till morning this time. He wasn't about to cater to its whims in the middle of the night.

Peter went into the bathroom, brushed his teeth, and drank an Alka Seltzer. Yawning heavily, happy that she had apparently tired of waiting and fallen asleep, he tried the bedroom door. It was locked.

"Oh, for the love of — not this again! Eleanor!" He gripped the doorknob, attempting to squelch both his voice and his anger and avoid waking his son upstairs.

There was no answer. A pain, like an electric current, surged through his temples.

"Eleanor!"

A moment of silence, and he stormed back to the kitchen, determined to spend the night at the table reading the newspaper. In the cupboard below the sink he found a bottle of Mogen David elderberry wine. He poured half a tumbler and flopped noisily into a chair. Glancing about for the newspaper, he noticed a folded red ribbon behind a potted vine at his elbow. Beneath the ribbon was a card. He read the front of it.

"Happy Birthday to Our Dear Daughter."

He opened it, skimmed the small, sentimental Hallmark poem, closed it again and took a drink of the wine. It was dismally sweet.

"So that's what is was," he mumbled. "Good show, Peter, old boy."

He took another drink, walked slowly to the bedroom door, and bent low to the keyhole.

"Eleanor. Listen, darling. I'm sorry. It completely slipped my mind. I've run myself ragged today. Please open the door, will you? I'll make it up to you tomorrow."

But as he said it, he realized that tomorrow was booked. He also recalled that his son had asked to go along to the retreat, but he'd forgotten to give him an answer.

A man can do just so much and no more, he thought. What do they expect?

"Eleanor, please answer me. I love you."

From inside came a dead voice. "I'm sick of you. Go sleep with your son."

"Eleanor—"

"Just go away."

"But—"

"Please!"

Peter rose, shuffled through the hall to the staircase. "These stupid games," he mumbled. As he mounted the stairs, the pain in his head increased. At the top he paused, looking across the small dormer room at his young son, sprawled sideways on the bed, his sheet knotted about him. Beside him on the floor was his Cub Scout pack, full and carefully belted shut, a canteen, his sleeping bag. Peter smiled. He went into the room. The air was hot to the point of being oppressive. No doubt Eleanor had taken the fan for herself. He stripped to his shorts and pulled back the covers of the extra bed. There were no sheets on it. The pillow was damp mattress ticking without a case; he punched it once with a closed fist.

"Dear God," he muttered. "Bless this happy home."

He went to his son and stood over him. The perfect order of the boy's equipment amused him. Just like his mother, he thought, and touched the freckled forehead.

"I can see you're determined to go along, old fellow," he whispered, reaching under the boy to straighten him out.

But at the touch his hand recoiled with revulsion. The sheet was soggy with urine. He returned to his bed, sat down on the edge, and held his throbbing head in his hands. What was the matter with that boy? Nearly nine years old and still this carry-on. Goodrich's pills were a bloody waste of money.

He wondered whether he should wake the boy and get him into dry bedclothes. But he couldn't recall where Eleanor kept the sheets, so he decided against it. "Honestly," he thought, "how can I take him on retreat when he pulls this sort of thing. He'll just have to sit it out this year, that's all."

Peter lay back on the bed, clutching his hands together at his chest. On the ceiling a large water spot stained the asbestos tiles. It formed the likeness of a human head, a female with wide, blank, pupil-less eyes. Incredible, he thought, it's exactly like Little Orphan Annie. He mused, faintly vexed that he'd never noticed it before. Then he began to pray aloud.

"Dear God, I ask you to give me strength in this time of crisis. I ask you to strengthen my wife to understand the great mission I have undertaken in your name. Give her patience and independence of spirit. Teach her to go her own way, to lean less on me when others require my strength. Help her to—"

He stopped mid-prayer. His son had rolled over and begun to whimper. Irritated at the interruption, Peter lay silent, staring at the water stain, till the boy quieted. For some reason, he found himself thinking of Mrs. Dunlap's maid.

"And dear God, help me to help poor Mrs. Howard," he continued. "Give me the power to reach out to all the afflicted and heal them with the breath of your spirit. All of this I ask in the name of your son, Jesus Christ. Amen."

And with a sufficiently unburdened spirit, he crawled beneath the coarse, petitpoint bedspread and fell swiftly to sleep.

Questions for Reflection and Discussion:

1. What is the implication of the pastor's name? Of his bleeding heel?
2. Why does Lucille Dunlap dislike "intellectual" sermons?
3. How does Mrs. Howard contrast with Mrs. Dunlap?
4. Why is this church group discussing a literary work? Why does Lockwood have them discuss this particular one?
5. Evaluate Peter's exegesis on John the Baptist. What motivates his interpretation?
6. Contrast the reactions of Henry Piper and Mrs. Much to the *Winesburg, Ohio* characters.
7. Discuss the meaning of the title in terms of Peter's closing prayer at Mrs. Dunlap's, and of the two paragraphs im-

mediately following that prayer.
8. What do Peter's attitudes and actions toward his cat, his wife, and his son reveal about him?
9. What is the predominant tone of this story?
10. What does this story expose about each one of us?

MERLE MEETER

Philosophy of Life

"So, personally, I have nothing against you, McKinnon. But I'm afraid we'll have to let you go." Rexwroth assumed his most sympathetic smile and pushed his heavy walnut chair back from his wide, cluttered desk. He was an extremely busy man, with teaching duties, dissertation committees to oversee, and the department headship. He wanted you to know how valuable his time was.

Will McKinnon attempted a smile in response, but he was still shaking. Not that his firing was completely unexpected. He looked down at his brown, soft-leather shoes, and then up at the diminutive gleaming redwood image from some aboriginal culture that sat front center on his superior's desk.

Rexwroth apparently felt compelled by the brief silence to say more. "As I said, McKinnon, you're a hard worker, and the students—most of them—like you. But we've got these two top-notch graduate assistants who fit perfectly into our program. Frankly, we're planning to drop the Augustine course. We may incorporate it—there simply aren't enough takers to justify it anymore."

"I can understand that, Dr. Rexwroth. I haven't built up much of a reputation, I realize."

Looking up quickly, Rexwroth leaned suddenly forward, his curly amber hair haloing the bald spot that glinted under the artificial light. "That's part of the problem, McKinnon. You *have* built a particular kind of reputation, even gathered a following of peculiarly — ah, religious, disciples, whereas philosophy is to be factual, objective, dispassionate, not emotive and subjective. In fact, that's why you received only another one-year contract for this year instead of — ah — something better."

Will caught himself about to reach under his sweater for a cigarette, then remembered that he had quit smoking some months before. What defenses had he left himself, he wondered.

"I try very hard to be objective and scholarly in my teaching, Dr. Rexwroth, including the presentation of my own perspective." It was too late now, Will knew. Why bother with this discussion? Rexwroth was probably laughing inside.

"That's precisely it, McKinnon!" The pedagogic index finger jabbed at him like a miniature air hammer. "You evangelize without even knowing it. Some of our best prospects are coming to me about it. In fact, they're getting confused about the very nature of philosophy!"

Relaxing somewhat, Rexwroth continued, "Knowledge, facts, science are one thing, young man. Religion and faith and presuppositions are matters of personal opinion, okay for private life, perhaps, but alien to the realm of higher education."

Will sensed his pulse rate rising and felt the sweat under his arms. He wanted to get away; his stomach was churning again. What would he say to Ginelle? They had a tennis date with Jason and his latest for three o'clock, and it was after two already. But he didn't have to reply, for Rexwroth was well into his subject now.

"You bring in these contemporary Christians, McKinnon, but they're simply not philosophers! T.S. Eliot and C.S. Lewis — they're just literary people. And Francis Schaeffer's nothing but an itinerant preacher with a popular, pseudo-intellectual approach."

He was being drawn into it again, and what good could it possibly do? He was out of a job, and Ph. D.'s were a dime a dozen — especially philosophers. Five hundred a month for a fancy apartment when they could have been buying a home for less. Maybe it was a good thing they *hadn't* bought.

Rexwroth gathered himself solidly, like a water buffalo preparing to charge. "Metaphysical man is dead, McKinnon.

European metaphysics is bankrupt! The evolutionary-empirical method is the only rational way for modern man."

"How about Jesus Christ, the way, the truth, and the life?"

"Now what in heaven's name does that have to do with philosophy?" Rexwroth could hardly modulate his tone. "You tell me how a simple Hebrew moralist could ever deal with the complex philosophical and ethical problems facing us today?"

Will McKinnon, sitting there in his light-blue sweater and brown corduroy slacks, felt once again like a candidate defending his thesis. Late March sunlight slanted in through the half-opened blinds and glanced off the gold Cross pen-and-pencil set in Rexwroth's lapel pocket. The man's chin jutted towards him as Will began to answer.

"Well, first of all, Jesus is the Christ, not a simple Hebrew moralist. He is the crucified and risen Redeemer, the King of creation. That's the basic difference in our perspectives, Dr. Rexwroth. And Colossians 1 says that in Christ all things cohere, have their integration." Will's words re-echoed ominously in the silence.

A vein throbbed in Rexwroth's forehead, but he settled back with a slow smile, as if he had merely confirmed a decision.

"McKinnon, you're no philosopher. You're a biblicist! Your wife teaches art here, doesn't she?"

"She's in drama—stage settings, costuming. . ."

"Well, you get yourself enrolled in a seminary. She can teach drama while you get your degree in theology. Preachers are really raking in big money these days. And with your gift of rhetoric and background in philosophy, you could proselyte much more effectively from a pulpit. Otherwise, it's a teaching job in some little church college or Bible school. A state university is certainly no place for sectarian views."

The chairman stood up and thrust out his hand across the great desk, directly above the little statue. Will rose awkwardly in response to accept the farewell handshake. His right leg was asleep, and he felt exhausted. "Thanks, Dr. Rexwroth. I'm sorry I disappointed you."

"Not everybody's cut out for this type of work. I'm just sorry that we couldn't have told you a month ago so that you could have—uh, started looking around earlier."

"That's okay. I appreciate your situation here. God bless you."

"Oh, yes—and good luck to you, McKinnon."

Their apartment was only three blocks from the campus, and Gin was sunning on the patio, her Wilson wood lying on the parquet beside her. Jason and his girl would be along in about fifteen minutes to pick them up. Usually, Will enjoyed tennis, though he wasn't quick enough to be a really good player. He had played number three singles on his high-school team but had been knocked out in the second-round tryouts at U. of C.

Will had never felt less like playing tennis. He pulled off his sweater and hung it in the closet. Then he went to the kitchen and shakily poured himself a glass of the orange juice left over from breakfast. Ginelle usually didn't bother to drink hers—or she skipped breakfast altogether. He felt like going to bed and sleeping all weekend.

He peeked through the kitchen window. Should he tell her before? Gin was beautiful, no doubt. A tall blonde with a figure like. . .who was that Australian gal?

Will slumped into a chair and sipped his orange juice listlessly. He'd had a cheeseburger for dinner and he sure wasn't hungry now. Yeah, Gin was a winner, all right. She figured that he was climbing into tenure just as she was. Now he was fired, and she loved her job and her dramatic friends. She wouldn't want to leave the University.

Ginelle came smoothly into the bedroom as he was tying his jogging shoes—he liked them for tennis. She stretched sensuously, laid her racket on the red-velvet bedspread, and did twenty full squats in front of the mirror, calves and thighs tensing fully. Will was used to this routine.

Breathing deeply after the knee-bends, she looked into the mirror and said, "Jay said three, and it's five minutes to. Have a good day?"

Will ducked into his closet for his T-3000. "I'm ready. Had a talk with Rexwroth. I'll tell you about it after tennis."

"Rexwroth? What happened—was it about your appointment?

Did you get it?"

"Not exactly."

"Another one-year?"

"Not that either." He stood up and tried a grin, but it came off badly.

"They couldn't have!"

"I'm afraid so."

Ginelle snatched up her Wilson and slammed it down on the bed. Dust motes swam up into the air. Will turned away and lifted his sunglasses off the frame of their wedding picture and hooked them over his brown-framed glasses.

"The dirty skunks! I suppose it was your Christianity?"

"Mostly that, I guess."

"And they say they don't have religious discrimination here!"

"Not if you don't teach according to your convictions." Will released some of his frustration.

"I wish you'd never started going to that church. We were much happier before. I told you to keep your Jesus out of the classroom. Christmas is the time for that—if you have to have a martyr to worship."

"He's alive, Ginelle!" Will faced her contempt.

"Oh yeah? What's he doing for you now, for *us?* We've got bills to pay, brother! Who pays the rent? Christ doesn't bring home any paycheck around here!"

Will just looked at her, but he felt hopeless. He understood exactly how she felt. She leaned toward him, statuesque and rigid with anger, but he picked up the can of new balls and started for the living room.

"I don't feel like arguing about it, Gin. We've already done too much of that. Tomorrow's Saturday. I can start writing applications—the Lord will find us something."

But she came striding after him. "Oh, it's all over, is it? What if I like it here? They want me to go on for my degree. I'm not letting you drag me down, Will!"

They both heard the car then. Gin went for her warmup jacket, while Will let the reverberations of Jason's knock subside before he went to the door. Jason never used a doorbell. With him was a bouncy little brunette, but Jason did all the talking. He was a tall,

rangy type, muscled like an offensive end or a basketball forward. For a moment he seemed to sniff the atmosphere warily,
but then he was laughing, his usual hearty self.

"Okay, ready, gang? Let's get going. You okay, Gin? You look a
little pale."

"I'm fine, Jay. Just a headache from the thinner. We painted
sets all morning. I need some fresh air."

"Great! Hey, this is Sue Wilkins—an old racketball buddy. We
met at the club last winter. Sue works at an insurance agency
downtown. Sue, Will McKinnon, the brilliant philosopher I told
you about, and Ginelle, who's at home on the stage."

Sue smiled, nodded, shook hands. "I'm happy to meet you. I
only hope my game is on." She was not awed by Jason's
breeziness.

"We can always switch partners if things don't work out,"
Ginelle responded, obviously not in a very good state of mind.

Will spoke quickly then, "Pleased to meet you, Sue. We
always have a good time. I'm no Connors either, so relax." He
didn't feel like being jovial, however.

"C'mon then! It's perfect tennis weather, seventy-two degrees!
The back seat of the Bird may be a mite cramped, but we'll crank
up the front one as far as possible." So Jason hustled them in,
dumped the gear in the trunk, and wheeled out toward the club
courts. Will wondered how Jason was as a psychologist. He
seemed too organized to be sympathetic.

Ginelle was unnaturally reserved all the way out to the suburbs,
so Will tried to hold up their end of the conversation. The whole
situation was making him uneasy.

As they warmed up, Will and Jason blasting backhands
crosscourt and the girls hitting on the next court, Will felt that
the beautiful spring day was a dream. The winter had been
dismal and stubbornly cold, with several blizzards, and this
Friday was really the first warm, windless day of the season.

Nevertheless, Will played mechanically. The shock of disappointment and Ginelle's response had numbed him. He concentrated on hitting the ball as deep as possible, for he couldn't
begin to power the ball as low and hard as Jason. Out of the cor-

ner of his eye, he watched the women rallying.

Gin hit hard too, and she liked to move to the net, but Sue was a scrambler and could throw up an accurate lob if she got in trouble. They seemed to be enjoying themselves—even Ginelle had loosened up and was finally complimenting a particiularly good shot by Sue. Yet, *he* was the Christian, and if God really did work out everything for the good of those who love Him, then *he* should have been the happiest person on the courts. Wasn't it Paul who had said, "Rejoice in all things"? Or was it "Give thanks in all things"?

The first two sets went to Jason and Sue, 6-4; 6-3. Jay's serves were untouchable, as usual, and whenever a lob fell a bit short, Jay went floating back to rifle it away with his favorite shot, the leaping overhead.

Ginelle wanted to change partners after the second set, so they switched, and Will and Sue went down fast, 6-1; 6-0. Only good net play brought them to deuce in several of the games, but they were consistently outgunned on the big points, and neither Jason nor Ginelle was the type to let up or to hit a shot that wasn't directed at an opponent's weakness.

As the fourth set ended, Will was near the net, backpedaling desperately as Sue's weak return of a Jason backhand popped just over the net. Blonde hair flying and eyes flashing, Ginelle moved in to smash the cripple at her retreating husband. Will got his racket up, clumsily, sideways, to protect his midsection, and the ball carromed off wildly. But the force of Ginelle's shot forced the other edge of the racket painfully into his groin.

He shook it off as best he could, but it had been too close for comfort. Seeing that Will was okay, Jason remarked cheerfully, "You almost nailed him that time, Gin!"

Ginelle reddened, high on the cheekbones, and muttered, "Sorry, Will."

"That's all right, Gin. It was a good put-away. Just like the books tell you to do it, right at the hip." So they all shook hands and headed for the clubhouse.

Will noticed that Ginelle was the only smoker. Jason was a

jogger and a health nut, yeast and molasses and wheat germ. Ginelle hadn't really started to smoke heavily until after one of Will's students, a graduate in the Augustine course, had invited them to his church one Sunday morning. That had been over a year ago. They had been attending together for several weeks, Ginelle grudgingly, when Will observed, "Gin, maybe this Jesus they talk about *can* help us with our problems."

Gin had answered irritably, "You get carried away, Will. You've got a touch of the fanatic in your make-up. *I* don't feel guilty or empty or frustrated. What crimes have we committed? And I've got so many interests I don't know what to take up next."

"That's just it," Will had said. "That's *your* frustration." Now he just felt guilty himself—about his glibness then. He knew that somehow he was responsible for the smoking that kept Gin nervous and self-critical. Or at least aggravated her problems.

It was comfortable in the lounge. Will tried to relax as Jason's confident voice flowed around them—the man had even played celebrity tennis. Sue was a good audience, Will noticed—and attractive! Gin appeared thoughtful and remote as her fingers tapped her cigarette or raised her glass. Will tried unsuccessfully to block out thoughts of Rexwroth and his own uncertain future.

Suddenly a question shattered his preoccupation. He heard his wife's words echo in the silence. "What would *you* do, Sue, if your husband was fired by the very university where you had made a life for yourself?" The question had been enunciated slowly, with premeditation.

Sue was speechless, so Jason filled in as smoothly as possible. "That's really tough, Will. I take it it's not hypothetical, Gin? It's something both of you have been anxious about for some time, isn't it?"

Now how could he have known that, Will wondered. Had Gin been talking to Jason as a counselor? She didn't have to account to him for her confidences, but this wasn't the first time, he suddenly recalled, that Jason had revealed extraordinary knowledge of their relationship. Jason was continuing, speaking reasonably and encouragingly.

"Surely there are other colleges with philosophy departments—
I mean colleges in commuting distance. And there must be
plenty of high-school positions available to someone with as
much education as you have, Will."

How typical of Ginelle when she really wanted to hurt
someone. Will struggled to answer calmly. "There's not much
philosophy taught in high school, Jay, even in the elitist schools."
Will spoke with a grimace and shivered slightly.

Then Sue, obviously trying to be helpful, suggested, "Couldn't
Will do some kind of pastoral counseling or something in that
line at your clinic, Jason?"

Ginelle just sank down a few inches and listened, graceful and
tawny as a lioness, looking suddenly content and smugly
detached, while the others probed fastidiously at the body she
had dragged into the open. As Will heard the futile proposals, he
wondered how Jason would handle Sue's embarrassingly direct
appeal.

"Well, we *have* thought on occasion of hiring a chaplain—but
Will's not really qualified as a minister, not seminary educated or
ordained, and so forth. Furthermore, not many people have
specifically religious problems, church-related, that is. I mean,
Will, here, is a philosopher, and a philosopher *per se,* it seems to
me, has no place in a clinic where we deal with practical real-life
problems."

Jason seemed to run down finally, uncharacteristically, and he
called for more drinks. Will was almost amused despite the
nausea he was beginning to taste. Maybe another drink *would*
settle his stomach. A little wine for the stomach. Or "Give strong
drink to him that is ready to perish."

Ginelle looked lovely and self-possessed now as she leaned
against the red-leather cushions and leisurely stirred her drink.
Will remembered how beautiful he had thought her when they
first met in the old University of Chicago library. Introduced by
Miriam—what was her last name, Wagner—they had been attracted to each other immediately. Often, lately, he had wondered why.

And Miriam had played cupid. He had co-edited the undergrad
lit review with her during his senior year—a philosophy major

who wrote free-verse poetry (why had he stopped so abruptly?) and an English major who composed morality plays. He smiled slightly.

They had made a great team. He was the agnostic, suavely cynical, easily renouncing a bland Presbyterian background. She was the evangelical Christian, with a quaint touch of mysticism, he recalled. Each was the other's most enthusiastic audience. And buddy Miriam had introduced him to one of her roommates just because she knew that both of them enjoyed tennis.

Everything had moved fast after that. Tennis dates, other dates, three more months of school, and an August wedding. Then two full years of grad school, grinding right through the summer vacations, and his degree—well, all but the dissertation, which he had completed during his first year of teaching at N.S.U.

And now after just two years of teaching, was his career over? Maybe he had glorified his position, made it an idol. When he became a Christian, he certainly hadn't dreamed that things could turn out this way. Attempting to obey God definitely had its hardships.

When he snapped back to his surroundings, Ginelle was laughing loudly at something Jason was telling them about a client who came in every week for an hour's conversation. But the guy played a different role each time, and he actually wrote and rehearsed his scripts for those fifty-dollar performances.

Ginelle was starting to lose control already after her second drink, so Will started getting ready to leave before things got too noisy—or messy.

"I'll get it, Jay. We should be going. I've got some papers to read tonight." But Jason was already signaling peremptorily for the bill.

"Sorry, folks, I forgot the time. Sue has to be home by six for an employer banquet. The boss is taking her out, right *Susan?*" He winked at Ginelle, who wasn't paying attention, so he switched his leer to Will, who tried not to act knowing. Sue deserved better than that; she seemed like a decent girl.

Jason dropped Sue off at her place, then continued toward the McKinnons' apartment. It had cooled off, and Ginelle was coming back to life. They all sat in the front seat of the Thunderbird. Very companionable Will thought wryly. The events of the afternoon already seemed years away, but he knew that their immediacy would return the moment he and Ginelle faced each other at the table or in their bedroom. It hadn't been going very well there either, both of them too busy, too preoccupied, too tired, too self-centered.

In fact, it had *never* gone especially well, he thought, knowing he was being unfair — not that he could call her frigid, but Ginelle had never learned to relax. Was that partly his fault? And now, especially, since he had tried to turn his life over to Christ, a real barrier had risen between them. Jealousy, hostility, fear surfaced in those Sunday morning arguments before he went to church, usually alone, or to a Bible discussion. Maybe he shouldn't have left her at those times, but he also needed the fellowship of those who served the Savior.

When Jason pulled up in front of their house, Ginelle surprised them both by saying suddenly, "Will, I'd like to talk to Jason alone for a few minutes, please. A professional, psychological matter, okay? I'll be right in. You just go on ahead."

It sounded foreboding to Will, so he said, affecting levity, "A husband should have the right to testify in his own defense, shouldn't he?"

But Jason waved him off airily. "It's okay, Will. She'll be only a minute. She probably wants to know how she should apologize for that last overhead."

Will was repulsed by the crassness of the comment, but he only said, "All right. Thanks for the tennis and the drinks, Jason." He thought of adding, "I'll put a roast in the oven," but he wouldn't beg. So he just took the rackets that Jason handed him, and walked stoically into the house.

He did set the table, however, and as it was more than a few minutes, he went into the living room. He couldn't resist a look through the front window. They were still talking, all right, sitting just as he had left them — or maybe even a little closer? He turned away angrily and began to crumple some newspapers to start a fire in the fireplace. A bed of twigs, a couple logs from the bucket, and a red-tongued fire was soon licking at the wood. He fell back into his favorite chair. Dusk was rapidly closing in, but he didn't feel like turning on any lights.

"Well, God, where are You now?" In his letters over the past year he had hinted to philosopher acquaintances in a few church-related colleges that he might be open to an appointment. But there had been no response; there was more firing than hiring in philosophy departments lately. Not that he was averse to other work, even manual labor. He checked off his capabilities: truck driver, gardener, factory worker, carpenter, mason's helper, mailman, farmhand, grocery clerk. That was about it, but it was enough. Oh, he could make a living, all right. But no fancy apartment or club tennis. And could he still hold Ginelle?

He stood up restlessly, took a few steps toward the kitchen, then got down and pumped out sixty pushups, paused at the top for two or three deep breaths, and forced out ten singles. He had once worked up to a hundred in college. There were advantages to weighing 175. Let Jason try to do seventy pushups at 215!

What was taking her so long? He went back to his chair to look into the fire, but suddenly lurched forward to squint at the darkening outlines of the car and its occupants. Were they embracing? He let out his breath with a snort. But he knew that he hadn't paid enough attention to his wife. He had ignored her moodiness, assuming that it was only temporary.

She was getting out alone. Jason was leaving. Again he released his breath, this time with relief. But he would just sit there in front of the fire and wait for her to come in. No use getting excited and running over to kiss her, though that's what he wanted to do.

He sensed that she would say exactly what she wanted to say this time, even though she might have hidden some things before. He knew her tight-lipped reserve, but he usually chose it over quarreling. Now he wondered whether that had been wise, the way of love. Was argument *really* the only other option?

Ginelle closed the front door, came into the room, and sat down on the sofa. She didn't turn on any lights either. They both looked at the fire for a minute without saying anything.

"Want to go out for dinner?" Will ventured. Pretty feeble, he thought, but better than nothing.

"Will, I've been seeing Jason for several months — more often than you realized, that is. It's been Platonic so far, though I guess that's not the right word after what you told me about Plato. First you become a Christian, and then you lose your job. I think I've made it clear that I don't want to lose mine. But that's only one thing — it's *all* been going from bad to worse in the last year. Will, I want out!"

It was warm in the firelit living room, but Will felt icy cold and suddenly hopeless. "Why, Gin, you've never even hinted at something this radical before. Can't we just sit here and quietly discuss —"

"There's too much we haven't discussed, and too much we have. And there's a lot more I don't even care to discuss. My parents never cared for this marriage. Will, I've made up my mind. I want a divorce."

"What would you do?"

"Jason says he loves me, and he wants to marry me as soon as we — as soon as these legal matters are taken care of. I believe him. As much as I believe anything. At least I'm willing to take my chances."

"I don't trust him, Gin."

"Will you contest it?"

"You're really serious, Ginelle?"

"Are you serious about being a 'born-again Christian'?"

"Yes, but that's hardly —"

"Then I'm just as serious about this. It's *my* life and *my* career and *my* happiness, right?"

"But I still love you, Gin!"

"*You* may call it that. I call it habit, routine, being only second or third on your list of priorities."

"I never realized you were this bitter."

"I don't like to grovel — and some things I don't talk about."

"Except to your psychiatrist."

"Right on, pal! I'll get my clothes packed and a few other things. You can have the rest. I've got my checking account. Jason will be around in an hour to pick up the stuff in his van. . .

Why don't you go to a movie or something? It would be a lot easier on all of us."

"Gin, can't we try it for a week or so? Remember those first months of our marriage when we didn't take so much time for all the other things?" He got up and began walking toward her, but she rose quickly and slid past him toward the bedroom.

"That's all in the past. The rosy romance of youth. I've grown up since I slaved for two years in that lousy library reference room to help you get that worthless degree. But I know my work now, and I like it. I also know what I'm worth!"

"You'll never be happy with him."

"Well, there sure hasn't been much joy around here! You must save it all for your Christians."

"You're right, Ginelle. And I'm sorry. I should have set aside more time for us to do things together. . . Would you, uh, consider talking this over with somebody like Vince Irwin?"

"He's an elder in your church, isn't he? No, no thanks, Will. I've been coming to this decision for some weeks. Today was just the straw. By the way, what do *you* plan to do? About the job, I mean."

They stood there confronting each other, both worn out by the controversy, ten feet apart in the darkened room, the firelight limning their faces. A movie might have them fall into each other's arms, but life didn't work that way. Maybe Sophocles was right: "Call no man happy until without sorrow he has passed the bound of life."

"What will *I* do? I have absolutely no idea, nor any interest in the subject," he replied tonelessly. "And you can do what you want, Gin. I won't try to hold you against your will."

"Thanks," she said shortly and turned away, almost too swiftly, toward the bedroom. Yet he knew how stubborn Ginelle was about anything she decided to do.

For the next week Will lived in a kind of dream. He went through the motions, taught his classes and evaluated papers like an animated computer, shaved once a day, sprayed deodorant through his T-shirt, ate in cheap restaurants, talked to no one, skipped church and Bible discussion, took walks to avoid answering the telephone, and went to bed every night before ten—not that he could sleep.

He did call Ginelle at Jason's on Tuesday evening, but a maid said that she wasn't there. If she was, she obviously wouldn't speak to him. On Thursday the divorce papers arrived. It was all over now—job and marriage.

Will felt sick with guilt and very near despair. He thought of some of Hopkins' sonnets, especially one that started, "No worse, there is none, pitched past pitch of grief. . ."—he didn't remember the rest. He had no awareness of the Holy Spirit, no sense of communion with Christ. He couldn't seem to work up the energy, or the faith, to speak to God, and God apparently wasn't bothering to speak to him.

Now it was Saturday night, and he was still drifting. He knew that he had lost about ten pounds because his pants sagged, but he didn't feel like boring another hole in his belt. Who cared anyway? The apartment was relatively clean, apart from dusting and vacuuming, but it was like a tomb. Was he the corpse?

He dropped a record on the hi-fi and sprawled on the davenport. Through the stupor of his self-pity he overheard some of the words. The melodies were quite familiar, but he found himself listening to the lyrics for a change: "And with His stripes we are healed. . . . Behold and see if there be any sorrow like unto My sorrow. . . . For the transgression of Thy people was He stricken. . . . Since by man came death, by man came also the resurrection of the dead! For as in Adam all die, even so in Christ shall all be made alive!"

After the phonograph snapped off, he lay for a long time motionless, until finally tears began to ooze out of his eyes and run down the sides of his face. He didn't even try to wipe them away. He couldn't recall the last time he had cried. When he thought back over all the persons he had been jealous of, hated, ignored, or otherwise hurt, ending with Ginelle, he suddenly brought his open hands hard against his face. "Lord God, forgive me!" he cried aloud. And like an echo to the cry the telephone rang.

He didn't want to answer it, but even thieves have felt compelled to answer the telephone. "Hello, Will McKinnon speaking."

A strangely familiar voice replied, "Hi, Will. How are you? This is Miriam Wagner."

"Miriam! Well, I'm fine—ah, that is. . . What're *you* doing now?"

"Teaching freshman rhetoric and the metaphysical poets at Wheaton—my third year here. How is Ginelle?"

"Probably better than I am."

"Say, I heard from a friend who goes to your church that you've become a Christian, Will."

"Well, yes, I guess so. But Gin isn't."

"What do you mean, 'you guess so'?"

"I've just been fired, and Gin is divorcing me. I'm not sure of much anymore."

Will began to wonder whether they had been cut off when Miriam said, "I'm really sad for you, Will—*and* for Ginny."

"I appreciate that, Miriam." Will tried to get himself together. "By the way, why the call?"

"Well, we've got a job opening in the philosophy department, and the chairman asked me to sound you out." She hesitated, as though she were about to say more, then added, "The professors here have to promise not to drink or smoke. As I recall, you smoke, don't you, Will?"

Will grinned somewhat ruefully at the receiver as he shook his head. "I gave up the habit, Miriam. As for the alcohol—well, I'm sure I can get along without it. I don't like the associations I have with it."

"Good for you! That will help. . ." Again, a pause.

Will blurted it out: "And now this divorce, right? What will that do to my chances?" He could hear the tenseness in his voice, and he was surprised how much he wanted another start.

"I can't answer that, Will. I don't know any of the details."

"Do you think I should still apply?"

"Do you think God is still alive?"

"Well, yes, I think I've had some evidence of that."

"Then maybe you'd better talk to *Him* about it. God bless you, Will, whatever you decide." And she hung up. That was like Miriam.

Questions for Reflection and Discussion:

1. What does the name Rexwroth suggest to you?
2. Why exactly does Will McKinnon lose his job?
3. Why does Will seem afraid to talk openly with his wife—why is he so evasive?
4. What does the tennis match reveal?
5. Why does Jason attract Ginelle?
6. Is Will's Christian commitment the only thing that makes this marriage break up?
7. Why does the telephone ring immediately after Will says, "Lord God, forgive me!" Do such things happen? Are they usual?
8. What Biblical teaching (see, for example, Romans 14) underlies the promise of some Christian teachers not to drink or smoke?
9. Should Will McKinnon be allowed to teach at a Christian college even though he has been divorced?
10. Have you ever experienced what you considered to be a tragedy or a great disillusionment? How did the Lord bring you out of it—or how is He beginning to do so even now?

LAWRENCE DORR

A Slow, Soft River

The girl was driving the car up the slope, bouncing over the ruts gouged out by the run-off; then stopping a second, she waved. The man and the boy didn't look up from loading supplies in an old wooden boat half floating on the Itchetucknee. The river was cold and clear and smelled of the fish that swam close to the bridge, their heads pointing upstream. They were silver or black, nothing in between, with tails going like slow metronomes.

The girl turned onto the highway. When the man heard the car crossing the highway bridge he lifted his hand and wiggled his fingers in farewell. The boy waded into the river. Hunching over the transom with the outboard, he looked like a stork fishing.

By next year, the man thought, he'll be taller than I am. The boy was sixteen and he forty-five.

"Daddy," the boy said, straightening up, "we are ready to leave now."

"Sam," the man called. "Sam."

From under the bridge a big, gaunt black and tan hound sauntered down to the boat. He had a false joint in his hip that made him drag his right hind leg. He came to the man and put his muzzle in his hand.

"Samuel," the man said. He felt love rising in him like a great shout that spread over the giant water oaks, the face of his daughter in the car framed by dark hair, her emerald eyes smiling goodbye, the wind on the pale green sea of the river with its island-pools of blue, his tall, strong son; and Sam. Sam who had been found two years ago in a Georgia swamp on the verge of death. He lifted his arms as if he wanted to breathe in the blueness of the sky.

"Praise the Lord," the boy said matter-of-factly. "Get in, Daddy."

"Do you feel it too?" The man was astonished as if the boy had suddenly spoken in Chinese.

"I don't know why I shouldn't. I'm normal."

They floated under the highway bridge, then shot through the culvert under the railroad tracks. There were some houses on the left bank, but nobody in them. The river turned and widened. A congregation of ducks bobbed on the ripples. They were white ducks with one blue-wing teal in the midst of them. Out of sight a heron sounded deep bass. The ducks tuned up. Then, as if the conductor had come in, there was a sudden silence. Sam stood up in the boat and, lifting his head, bayed.

"That was an otter," the boy said. Some turtles plopped into the water, one after the other. Sam lay down again.

"I feel the same as when I listen to Bach," the man said. "I am lifted up, I am soaring, and I am almost bursting with joy. . . . But it is all orderly."

"You can't orderly-burst-with-joy," the boy said.

"We better crank up." The man was looking ahead where the Itchetucknee ran into the Santa Fe. There was a large object caught in the turbulence, coming up and going under again like a drowning man.

The engine started with a shriek, then the boy slowed it down to a pleasant purr. They went around the obstacle. Close up it was only a tree trunk that turned with a nice even speed. A roller in a well-oiled machine.

The Santa Fe was wider and darker and so swollen that it hardly moved between the banks of moss-covered trees. The boy speeded up. Two long waves left behind by the boat rushed the banks like charging cavalry, then broke up into shiny fragments among the tree trunks. Dry land was nowhere in sight. The man turned his head to the other side. A new charge just broke among the trees, flashing here and there like pieces of broken mirror.

Without warning he saw his friend Stefan on the hospital bed with his eyes half closed as he had been the last six weeks, breathing through a hole in his neck, his chest heaving. Then the sun came out, illuminating the spaces among the trees. The green patent-leather leaves of a huge magnolia reflected the light upward.

A garment of praise for the spirit of heaviness, he thought.

The boat changed direction, then got back on course. The boy had just finished taking off his shirt.

"Aren't you cold?"

"I wouldn't have taken it off if I were," the boy said.

"Vanity," the man said. "You want to get tanned, somebody else wants to bleach out. It's all vanity."

"If we all have it, you must have it too, Daddy."

"I have it moderately. On some Sundays when it is cold enough to wear my suit which I got to go to England in, I think, aha, not bad at all, but your mother will say: 'It's all right if you don't put on any more weight.' And I quit saying 'aha' till next winter."

"I remember when you bought that suit. I was five years old."

"That can't be."

"It was when I was starting school in England."

"And I am still not famous," the man said, "but at least I can get into my old suit."

"You look great in it, Daddy."

The man accepted this with a slight bow. He remembered how he stood in the door of the intensive-care unit not knowing if he should go in, conscious of his good suit and the nurses who were looking at him. But it didn't last long, this male pride, because he saw Stefan and understood that the rhythmic clicking he heard came from a green plastic pump attached to a hole in Stefan's neck. Stefan was pale, his unseeing eyes half open. For a crazy moment he had almost expected Stefan to ask him to have something to eat or to drink wine. He always did. But there was nothing other than the sudden awful silence of the pump. He was holding his own breath, wanting to share the pain; then the pump started and Stefan's chest expanded. The rhythm of the pump was back for a while, then it stopped again. He had reached out and laid his hands on Stefan's head.

"Do you want to fish?" the boy was shouting over the noise of the outboard. "Now that the sun is out I can see the fish." He cut back the engine.

"They prophesied rain," the man said, "but it doesn't look like it. . . . I'll just sit and watch you fish."

They anchored under a large oak. The boy cast; the bait falling like a meteor plopped into the river. Sam checked the sound. The boy reeled in and cast out again. Some ducks came in over the trees and settled on the Santa Fe.

"It's good to be away from the world," the man said.

"This is the world, Daddy." The boy reeled in again.

"I am glad that at least Sam can't talk back," the man said. "I am talking about this place where we can see and smell the sun."

"Yes," the boy said.

"I think it's all right for us to be here."

"Why wouldn't it be all right? We can't do anything for Stefan except pray."

"Even so, I saw Stefan at the nursing home and you didn't. There is no pump beside his bed now and that awful clicking is gone, but in a way it is worse. He struggles for each breath, and when I squeezed his hand there was nothing. In the hospital at least he squeezed back and I always thought of it as Stefan in a sunken submarine answering my knock, saying: 'I am here, I am here, I can hear you.' "

"I looked it up," the boy said, putting on his shirt. "The veins contract first to prevent too much bleeding, but if they don't relax after a certain time that part of the brain dies."

"Stefan was just lying there sweating," the man said, not smelling the sun, the river, and the fishes anymore, "and his pillow showed the damp outline of his head."

"I don't want to think of him that way," the boy said. "I always see him playing golf standing on that very green grass." He cast, the line flying out toward the other shore with a satisfying sound. The man saw Stefan, but he wasn't playing golf. He was sitting in his living room, in his dark green armchair next to a large candlestick with papers strewn around him on the carpet. Just two hours before the stroke.

"No bother at all," Stefan said. "While I read it you eat something. And have some wine."

"I have a nibble," the boy whispered. He leaned forward tensely, watching his line. "It's a bite, real heavy."

Play it, the man wanted to say, but he didn't say anything. The boy was a fisherman; he wasn't. He remembered his own fishing in the Danube with a cane pole and the dozens of fingerlings he pulled out from its olive-colored water. He also remembered his father's smile that said: this is all right for a little boy but men, our kind of men, hunt.

"A fighter," the boy shouted, reeling in and letting out the line again. "A fighter." The fish leaped clear of the water, then went down making the reel scream like an ambulance. "I am pulling him in now," the boy said. He turned the reel, his torso leaning forward in the attitude of a Protestant at prayer.

"I'll help you land it," the man said.

"I can manage, thank you." He stood up and lifted the fish into the boat. The fish, it was a bass, fell to the floorboard with a thud. The boy took out the hook. The bass kept on flapping on the board, then lay still. The man was watching its gills pumping in and out, in and out.

"Let's turn it loose," the man said.

"Why? It's a perfect eating size. It must be at least five pounds."

When the boy was younger, he cried easily. The look he gave now was a man's incredulous stare. I couldn't tell him, the man thought. Besides it would be all wrong. Pagan. An exchange with the god of the river.

The fish flopped once, then lay still. Suddenly it lit up as if a light had been turned on inside it.

"It's beautiful," the boy said. "It gave a good fight."

By carefully navigating among the cypress knees and tree trunks, they reached the shore under a bluff. In the silence of the switched-off outboard the tea-colored waves sounded like heavy breathing.

"I like to look down on the Suwannee," the man said. "This is how a flying heron sees it."

The boy laughed. "A two-hundred-pound heron. You would

need a steel reinforced kingsize nest."

The bluff's floor was flat and covered with dry grass and the contorted trunks of live oaks. Sam checked out the place by circling around it. The man set up the tent. The boy chopped wood, built the fire, then neatly arranged his cooking tools on a stump.

"How do you feel about fish soup?" he asked.

"With plenty of paprika," the man said. He walked down to the edge of the bluff and looked down on the Suwannee. Its color alternated between royal blue and green with the edges saffron. There were no boats going in either direction. Some ducks dove, then bobbed back to the surface. Sam came to stand against the side of his knee.

"Sam thinks this is a good place," the man said. He saw Stefan's saffron-colored shoes that he still wore even after shaving off his guardsman mustache and returning to his more conservative look. "I might get a crew cut," Stefan had said. "That would make me avant-garde now." But he didn't. His hair was damp and matted on the pillow. "A nice full head of hair," the nurse had said.

"Do you want to taste the soup, Daddy?"

It tasted perfect and he slurped another spoonful. "Who is to put a price on the joy of sitting here tasting your fish soup?"

"Some rivers had to be dammed up because people needed electricity. You can't damn progress, Daddy."

"I don't. I wouldn't be here without it. I was pretty badly shot up in the war. It isn't that at all."

"We can eat now," the boy said.

"Anything for Sam?"

The boy gave the dog a few uncooked hot dogs. The man watched the dog. When Sam ran he looked perfect. Only walking and sitting showed his crooked hip joint. We are both here, the man thought. It could have ended for Sam in that swamp in Georgia and for me at the border, under the barbed wire.

"Benedictus, benedicet."

"Deo gratias," the boy answered.

After washing up, the man climbed back up the bluff. He put the cooking utensils away and sat down on the blanket in front of the tent. For the last six years he and the boy had left on their annual boat trip on the Thursday before Easter. They would have a service of their own and be back at church on Easter Day. But this time it was different. He couldn't wait another day and he needed the strength of his son. The boy was whole while he was bruised and battered, only hoping to be made whole. The boy knew that with God everything was possible; he only hoped.

"John," the man said, "let's have our service today. It's because Stefan . . . we are out here and he —"

"I thought about it," the boy said. He stepped into the tent, got the prayer book, and sat down on the blanket.

"You read," the man said. "I left my reading glasses at home." He loved to hear the boy read, and besides, his own accent made him uncomfortable knowing that it would ruin something precious. The boy opened the prayer book.

"Now before the feast of the passover, when Jesus knew that his hour was come that he should depart out of this world unto the Father, having loved his own which were in the world, he loved them unto the end —"

The man listened, already thinking of tomorrow when He would be led to Pilate and shame and rejection and torment so that he, sitting here on a dog-smelly blanket, could be made clean and whole again.

" — For I have given you an example, that ye should do as I have done to you." The boy closed the prayer book. "Lord, we lift up our friend Stefan like those men who took the roof apart so that You could see their friend. You know what to do. We don't. Thank You."

"Amen," the man said, feeling peace carrying him along like a slow, soft river. He knew that he didn't have to worry about Stefan anymore.

The boy put away the prayer book in the tent and came back with a cigar.

"I didn't know that you were smoking. That cigar's at least six months old."

"I don't," the boy said. "Stefan taught me to blow smoke rings. They would float beautifully out here."

This time the man didn't ask the boy if he felt it too. He looked at his watch. It was four-thirty.

Just before dusk, the boy, who was fishing sitting in the tied-out boat, called him. There was a snake swimming across the river from the other side.

The rain began at noon Friday, and it was still raining when they pulled out the boat at Fannin Springs. The wood around the boat ramp smelled like mushrooms. There were cars crossing the battleship grey bridge at long intervals, messengers from another civilization. In the pause the only sounds were the rain splashing on the Suwannee, the river itself, and Sam's running on the wet leaves.

The boy was stacking up the camping gear with an economy of movement. He had done this so many times that he could do it with his eyes closed. The man was standing facing the bridge, waiting. He was happy. The trip was accomplished, to be cherished and savored in detail and compared to other trips till next year when another would be added. He was waiting for his wife to come with the car and boat trailer, waiting with the same gratefulness to catch a glimpse of her face as he had waited long ago in an English church. There was peace in this waiting, a healing where nothing of the bigger world intruded so that when in time he would turn on the car radio he would not be crushed by the hate and despair.

"Here she is," he said. The car rumbled across the bridge, the empty trailer bouncing behind it. The trip was over. "John, go and back it down for her."

He watched them embrace; then the boy got in the car, turned it around, and backed it down. She was walking toward him with Sam, who had joined her. In his happiness he didn't notice the tightness of her face, only that she was glad to see him.

"You haven't changed," he said.

"Why would I change in two and a half days?" She put her arms around him. "You smell like a wet dog."

They loaded the boat and the gear and were off. It began to rain harder, coming down in grey sheets. The bridge rumbled under them, then they were on the highway. The boy was talking, telling about the trip from the beginning — the way they shot through the culvert under the raliroad bridge and about the flock of ducks with one blue-wing teal in the midst of them. When he came to the fish he caught, the man remembered Stefan.

"How is Stefan?" he asked, interrupting the boy. He wasn't worried about him. He asked almost out of politeness. Even when she touched his arm he wasn't prepared for anything.

"He is dead," she said.

He heard the boy say "no" and his own fist crashed down on the steering wheel. The pain in his hand was the only feeling he had in the general numbness until he began to think and anger filled him against himself, against the river, against Thursday when at four-thirty he and the boy sat on a bluff hearing and feeling and trustingly celebrating like two madmen in the wine cellar of a bombed-out house. Then everything stopped. He drove on, peering through the windshield, noticing the curve in the road, an abandoned shack, a forlorn cow with her calf at her side. He marveled at himself that he could go on driving when life had lost all meaning because if Stefan was dead then God was dead also or He never had been in the first place and he had lived his own life for the past twelve years in a mental ward, hallucinating. There never had been a dialogue, a blessing and saving, a Body and Blood, and he was alone in an existential nightmare.

"There was no way I could contact you, and Jane wouldn't let me anyway," she said. "The women were in the room praying when suddenly Stefan sighed and relaxed. He was gone. He died on Thursday at about four-thirty."

Relief came with a rush and with it the accustomed and bearable seasons of joy and sadness all marching toward glory that was and is and ever shall be.

"Forgive me," he said. He began to cry.

Questions for Reflection and Discussion:

1. What contrasts in imagery are evident in the structuring of this story?
2. Why does the son seem so much more at ease with himself

and with God than does the father?

3. What was the father's relationship with Stefan, and how is that symbolized?

4. How does the fish caught by the son relate to Stefan?

5. Give several examples of similes and metaphors used skillfully in this story.

6. What is the significance of the "snake" and the "rain" which appear directly after the prayer?

7. Is the time span of the story meaningful?

8. Where is the reference to the title in the story itself, and what is its meaning in that context? Does the title also have another meaning?

9. Why is the time "four-thirty" crucially important?

10. As the story ends, a grown-up man begins to cry. Discuss whether the conclusion is sentimental romanticism or Christian realism.

PAUL BORGMAN

Wilbur Finds His Home

Just around the corner the white walls would become flourescent white, echoing cleanliness. But not godliness, thought Wilbur. Strange that those ever same white walls of smoothed-out concrete blocks could give back the sound of cleanliness. Smell, yes, but sound? Sound it did, though, as sure as the foaming cleanser of Ajax ever went boom boom. Especially now, as Wilbur stealthily approached the corridor junction. The wide gleaming halls of the nursing home filled the old man with fear and disgust and sometimes with excitement.

Behind Wilbur were the sweet chemical smells of shadowed balm. At times — mostly Tuesdays through Saturdays — Wilbur let himself be comforted by that peculiar ease. The old man felt bad about feeling so good in his little clean shelter.

His room was tucked around a corner in one of the few cul-de-sacs of the nursing home. So short was the little turn-off that no overhead fluorescent had been put up. Escaping light from the major corridor around the corner was all Wilbur needed as an invitation for his rare and carefully planned escapades beyond 21-A.

But never during hours. And never on Sunday. Sometimes Wilbur imagined that these catchy phrases now totally governed his eighty-year life. He could hardly remember the movie, but never on Sunday had never left him. The problem of roving Sunday visitors, of course, added to Wilbur's desire to keep counsel only with himself on this First Day. A lapsed Catholic, this was another of the old man's pet phrases: the evolution of Sunday's elevation. Alone, Wilbur reflected and planned—or dreamed in such a way that the necessary Monday action would be clear by Monday morning. Now for the first time he would get some Monday night ice cream. Sundays and Mondays were the only deliberate days of Wilbur's week.

Yesterday it struck him that this present venture was a matter of obtaining the one food in the entire nursing home that did no harm. Maybe even good. Wilbur chuckled. But still it was true—the only possibly healthy food in the entire nursing home.

Just ahead was the familiar corner, seven years' worth of familiar. Still, he had to be careful. Here in the short dead-end shadows of his permanent retreat, Wilbur could be stealthy without pretending his emphysema shuffle. Once in the colorless white of the clearly lit halls, cautious stealth would have to be implemented by the guise of a poor, worn-out man, stopping to catch his breath. He knew every line in this section of the wall, including the minutest details of the utility closet, the only other cavity besides his room in this end-of-the-road tunnel.

At first Wilbur left 21-A at 11:30 Monday nights only to squat against the cool end wall. Motionless and undisturbed, he became part of the shadows and the slight chill. These times had given him the emphysema inspiration. Cavities of all sorts impressed the old man with their air-holding capacity, and these Monday night squats usually ended with thoughts about the air in his head. As a child Wilbur had often pictured the dome of starry sky as a head—if adults were right and this space had no end, perhaps the head of God himself. He had been perfecting the winded feeling for so long that he wondered at times why the fake emphysema wasn't real. Only the gentlest of hints had been given the nursing home staff. Their threats of diagnostic tests frightened Wilbur at first, until he realized that the threats were as unreal as the emphysema. Wilbur's fear that wind-disease would someday be his lot scared him worse than the original diagnostic threats. Yet, he had to admit, he also felt at home with the winded state. Strange. Like fearing to be at home in this nursing home, and yet being at home—at least Tuesdays through Saturdays.

Slowly, softly, the old man emerged from the darkened turn-off, assuming now his shuffle-footed stealth. Wilbur would have to make it to the kitchen. During the first two years at the nursing home, Wilbur had volunteered his services in the kitchen. A big mistake, for two reasons — one of which became clear only many months after his retirement from service. First of all, the old man discovered that he was tolerated, not appreciated. This alone wouldn't normally have deterred the stubborn Wilbur. Months after he quit voluntary kitchen aid, he discovered the more important reason for his quitting. He had hated the loud bellowing mouth which forced the residents to a gutless fare. He had worked in the mouth. Huge molar cavities filled with steaming mounds of potatoes becoming mush; clanging jaws that pressed out biscuits and pastries; front teeth that shoved the goodness out of carrots, apples, and even beans; and the tongue of steam which forever mushroomed within the warm kitchen, turning smells and substance over and over. Then he would escape the mouth to eat its offerings.

Leaving kitchen aid had led to an alarming loss of weight. The nurses and staff talked to Wilbur. And finally Wilbur's son and his family had discovered something to say during their monthly visits. Only now the visits had to be on Saturdays instead of Sundays — another thing the family would like to talk about, Wilbur guessed. Seven years in this home, thought Wilbur, and the last five with the new visiting schedule. And still that silly Todd and his sillier wife and those abominable children can find nothing to talk about. Eighty going on ninety — maybe they think I'll live forever so there's time!

Actually, Wilbur did not will to lose weight. He just couldn't find anything to eat anymore. In the past five years the old man's taste buds had agreed with very few foods. Ice cream was one.

Every Thursday afternoon, upon the arrival of the Ladies Guild of the Grovetown Presbyterian Church, the one-hundred-plus residents of Grovetown Home for the Aged — and their staff — gathered in the dining hall for a religious variety show followed by neapolitan ice cream and vanilla thins, except when scout cookies were in season. Wilbur was not used to Presbyterians, but he rather enjoyed the programs. And he loved ice cream. Sometimes he honestly feared a return to childhood. Then the whole last seven years would make sense, being here and all. These ladies seemed willing to offer their childish busyness as a sacrifice for this fear—or perhaps their own, Wilbur occasionally mused. For the last four years he had sat at these Thursday-afternoon programs with Mrs. Grantfer. Mrs. Grantfer liked not quite so much ice cream, and only the strawberry. Wilbur liked a bit more ice cream, and only the chocolate and vanilla. And he liked Mrs. Grantfer.

Halfway to the nurses' head station, vacated at 11 P.M., except on Fridays, Wilbur's thoughts competed with the echoes of cleanliness bouncing back and forth between the white walls, straight through his little bald head. My little bald head, thought Wilbur, a skull with air, someday and maybe now. And these bad sounds of cleanliness, the ominous roar of Hell's void.

Wilbur was at the nurses' station now, a transmitting tower in a nervous system with upsetting signals of safety and whiteness reverberating up and down the arteries of the nursing home. The station was unmanned, which helped Wilbur not a whit. Always he approached with the trembles.

To make matters worse, the open-air office was at one of the two main junctions of the home. These junctions were the elbows of two large *L's* placed together with the long arm of the *L's* joined to form a straight line. The kitchen was at that middle joint, a swelling in the architecture which included the dining hall and separated the men's half of the home from the women's. Even the married's, thought Wilbur with a grin. Two wives had come and gone for Wilbur, both in the space of just twelve years. One died in first childbirth—along with the child. The second lasted for four years before leaving with their one son. She had left because Wilbur was silly—Wilbur grinned at the thought. And with Wilbur she had felt lost. What had she meant? Anyhow, the old man supposed she had found herself, and seriousness, because all he ever heard of her was from the miserable son who would be visiting from a Chicago suburb next Saturday. She had been in Chicago for these close-to-fifty years. The past was transformed into a Hail Mary full of grace as Wilbur peeked, in his perfected shuffling manner, around the corner. Something moved.

Wilbur shrank back and took stock. It was a receding human figure, too pleasantly ample in the bottom to be male, too unprofessionally dressed to be staff. Disappearing into the dining hall, it must have been. He peered again and all was silent. No doors were open, no shadows anywhere.

Hanging back, Wilbur glanced inside the closed-off portion of the nurses' station. For close to three years now, the Monday-night excursions had ended here. At first they were for fun, and then for business. Wilbur had been a pawn shop operator for his last thirty-seven years before Grovetown Nursing Home, in a neighborhood on Chicago's south side — just north of the colored area. He loved open-air markets, and pawn shops came close. Besides, pawn shops were year around.

This station reminded the old man of a small open-air shop. Along with his fear of this spot had come a desire approaching lust. Having learned in his trade to pick locks, Wilbur finally forced Sunday's imagination to the reality of Monday night lock-picking in this open-air market. For over two years he had been investigating and learning and even thieving. All the chemical properties and effects of pills, for example, were mastered, and some pills taken, others substituted. Wilbur always stayed an exact five minutes.

Who had belonged to that ample bottom? Wilbur could only think of Mrs. Grantfer, mostly because Wilbur never thought about any of the other ladies. Also because he often thought about Mrs. Grantfer. And Mrs. Grantfer had an ample bottom. Wilbur approached the corner once more. All clear, and very, very clean. Hell's void, the booming of no-sound. And no shadows.

From the nurses' station to the swinging dining hall doors, Wilbur hardly thought. Why? The trip was uneventful — something to think about next Sunday, he managed to think before the door swung shut behind him.

Careless, Wil, careless, letting a door swing like that. But here there were shadows. Wilbur slipped over to their table, Mrs. Grantfer's and his, and sat down for a moment. The little bald head was eased onto table-resting arms. It was that same feeling from the first annual all-state high school band—that initial sweep, as a group, through all those individually rehearsed numbers . . . surrounded by full glorious sound, and then the hush. Wilbur always felt that he had peaked too soon in life.

Slowly Wilbur filled with music from long ago as he remembered Mrs. Grantfer's smell. Leather goods from his pawn shop were in that smell, too. Of all the items pawned and then left those many years, Wilbur had been most shy but most fond of gun straps, holsters, grand old chairs, luggage, briefcases, purses, and even wallets. They all had that personal smell of leather. He could never understand how people could part with these, but he was always grateful. Sometimes for long minutes Wilbur would examine, touch, and finally smell. At those times something heavy would lift, and something light would leave to do good in the world. These were times when music and silence were heard. And occasionally Wilbur would let his face fall on the leather. All that wasted air in the cavity of his brain would become the wispy yet earthy wind sounds of oboe and bassoon and English horn. Then Wilbur knew that he was alive, and that he might always be, and that even God might be, actually be.

Raising his little bald head, the old man knew what he must do. That this had not been carefully worked out during Sunday ruminations would normally have deterred Wilbur. But not tonight.

Through the beckoning shadows Wilbur glided, aware that he would no longer need either stealth or his stealthy emphysema shuffle. Ever. From the huge freezer came the five-gallon tub of French vanilla. Later Wilbur would wonder why he hadn't chosen the butter pecan, his favorite. Two bowls from the long stacks of dishes were quickly filled. Two spoons from the open utensil counter, two fresh dish towels instead of napkins, and finally the eager woosh of the freezer door, a sweet amen of woosh.

Never before had Wilbur even had a glimpse of the women's section. But he knew without thinking that locating Mrs. Grantfer's room would be no problem. Once, on a summer afternoon's walk, he had gone by her window and gotten his closest look at the much-talked-about flower box. Almost every room had a box, but Mrs. Grantfer was known to have the knack of arrangement. Wilbur had only dared a glance, but he had sniffed to his heart's content. Now, seven doors down, he stopped before a simple but handsome cross. Mrs. Grantfer was appallingly religious, with no shame about her wonderful Lord. Nevertheless, her voice would dance as if she were in on something. Wilbur always suspected that she had owned a leather shop. Besides, she had her own very special smell. Many many Sundays Wilbur would try to locate that smell in his resting head, and always there came a sense of things remembered, but also of things out of reach. Beyond the Monday-night corridor junction, perhaps.

Wilbur stood, a bowl of ice cream in each hand. Then steps, and an open door, and the twinkling wise grin of Mrs. Grantfer.

"Why, Mr. Wilbur."

"Oh, I was just going to knock. . . ."

"With a bowl of ice cream in each hand?"

"Yes. Well, it's French vanilla, and. . . ."

"That's simply fine."

Wilbur had nothing to answer, so he put the bowls on a glass-topped coffee table at the foot of Mrs. Grantfer's bed. How can you fit a coffee table in these rooms, thought Wilbur, taking careful deep breaths. Discreet inhalation was Wilbur's way of looking around the room.

"Is that your emphysema, Mr. Wilbur? And I should think so, wandering about at this hour! Do your lungs adjust better by these after-hour tours? Strange. I know that's so. Here, you've given me too much ice cream."

Wilbur had finished his without a word, listening and smelling and getting a bit dizzy. He would go now, but they would leave together, someday. He'd get caught, tonight. Mrs. Grantfer would get caught. They'd have to leave. Maybe the Presbyterian ladies would help. Wilbur was feeling confused but very sure of himself. He knew it would be OK to ask her.

"May I smell you, Mrs. Grantfer?"

"Well. You're certainly close enough, Mr. Wilbur."

And so Wilbur discovered the godliness of Mrs. Grantfer. His head rested on her shoulder as they held each other. Wilbur stared at the tapestried wall. Warm blurs gathered for the first time in many years as Wilbur let his eyelids drop into the healing streams. What is this, Wilbur wondered. Another discovery had been made, a new question for Sunday. What is this? And where does it lead?

Questions for Reflection and Discussion:

1. What kind of person is Wilbur? Is he senile?
2. What is emphysema? Does Wilbur actually have it, or does he only pretend to?
3. Examine the metaphorical references to the kitchen as a mouth—what is the author trying to convey by this imagery?
4. What does the cleanliness of the nursing home come to mean for Wilbur and why?
5. In which paragraph does the author first provide substantial exposition (background information) on the main character, and what does it reveal about him?
6. Notice the many sights, sounds, and smells that are important to Wilbur. Why is this?
7. How does the author relate leather and musical sounds to God within the protagonist's mind?
8. Why do you think that Wilbur likes Mrs. Grantfer so much more than he likes anyone else—for example, his relatives?
9. Explain the final paragraph of the story in terms of Wilbur's discovery.
10. How does a story like this differ from a supervisor's report on the operation of a nursing home?

THE PARABLE

The parable is a literary form that tells a simple story of usually commonplace happenings, but it suggests a deeper level of meaning. Our Lord's parables were constructed to reveal the nature and requirements of the Kingdom of heaven, both by positive example and by contrast. The characters in such stories are generally everyday, typical folk, although some of the settings may be exotic.

Not every detail of a parable has a deeper meaning, however. But the artful parabolist frequently implies more than a single thematic or plot parallel, even though such a concentrated focus is his principal design.

The following contemporary parables present in lively narrative and realistic, colloquial dialogue the same sorts of inescapable and antithetical alternatives that Christ illustrated for us in His stories almost twenty centuries ago. To obey God or not to obey Him—that is the issue in the Christian parable. "If you love Me, keep My commandments!" said the King; and these brief narratives remind us of the ramifications of that calling for us today. Half hidden, too, is the joy of the redeemed life.

The tone in these works varies from the comic to the satiric, but the messages are alike serious and thematically significant. Interpretation, of course, is a major part of the fun, and this literary form particularly requires our thoughtful application.

MIKE VANDEN BOSCH

The Good Samaritans

Williger had been shot while walking through a skinned cluster of trees on one end of a sandy park called Williger's playground. There were, of course, no witnesses — not in Pearl City. They were more sophisticated than that. So the shot which killed Williger raised no more eybrows than would the slam of a neighbor's door.

Williger's body lay on the sand facing the sky. A plump mother joggled up pushing a Gerber's baby in a shiny stroller. She was staring at nothing. Then she zeroed in on Williger's body just a few feet in front of her.

"Oh oh," she murmured. She shook off a shudder.

"Mommie, man got owwie," squealed the child, pointing a pink, sucked-on finger.

"Ye-e-e-s. Bad, bad owwie," agreed the mother. She left her stroller and flicked a blackbird from the man's chest.

"Mommie, man needs a band-aid," said the child.

"Ye-e-s, big, big band-aid," said the mother, nodding. "Better call the police, don't you think?" She looked to the child for approval as she returned to the stroller, but the child appeared to be thinking. They left Williger lying on the sand.

The next lady came with her grey, neatly trimmed poodle, which had escaped from her dog-walker. So she, with her chauffeur, had driven out in search of the darling. She had spotted her dog in the middle of the sandy park, so while her chauffeur spun the Cadillac around the block, she hiked cross-park on high heels. When she had caught up with her poodle, it led the way to Williger's body. This she resisted though, saying, "No, Andrew Jackson, just up to the tree."

But Andrew Jackson had gotten within reach of the body and was lapping something from the hollow of the man's neck. The sound of the lapping tilted her head until she saw the body on the ground.

"No! No! Andrew Jackson. Dirty Dirty." She milked the droplets from the dog's whiskers with her silk handkerchief, then stood up and hurried away, cuddling her poodle. "Poor Andrew Jackson," she was murmuring as she left to inform the Park Director.

Soon after, a neatly dressed man with a neatly dressed son came walking by. "Life is a process of learning to adjust," the father was saying to his son. "That's what I was always taught."

"Look, Daddy, over there!" cried the son.

"What? What do you see?" queried the father, still talking about life-adjustment.

"There. Up ahead by the tree. A man's sleeping." The boy let go of his father's hand and ran ahead, his father following in his footsteps. "One must adjust to adverse situations with poise and resolution," the father was puffing as he came to Williger's side.

"Looks bad," he said, as he knelt beside the body. His son sat on one knee beside him.

"The man's been shot, see?" pointed out the father. "But there's no need to get excited. He'll be all right. Or at least comfortable," he added.

"Who did it, Daddy?" asked the son.

"We don't know, son," responded the father, bringing a thumb and forefinger to his chin. He adjusted his thoughts to objects. "See the BB's in his cheeks? Must have been a shotgun from close up. Hit him right here," he concluded, pointing.

"What's this, Daddy?" asked the boy, pointing to a protruding object hanging where the ear should have been.

"That's his eyeball, son. Did you know that our eyes are really round like . . . like marbles?" The man looked up for a moment. Again this vague feeling came over him, the feeling that he should probably call someone. Meanwhile his son put something into his shirt pocket.

Looking down at the body again, the father took out his white handkerchief. "I better cover the man's face," he said to his son. "We must always cover dead bodies." The red stains spread like a grass fire to the hems.

The father had a sudden inspiration—the solution. "We had better call a mortician," he suggested, taking the boy's hand and backing away. "They fix up dead bodies so that they look just like new. C'mon son," he said, "we've no time to waste." As he spoke, he looked down at his son and noticed that his son was peeking into his shirt pocket. The bulging pocket blotched with red stopped the father in his tracks.

"What have you got there, son?"

The son pressed the shirt pocket shut with his hand. "Nothin."

"Let me see." He pulled the son's hand from the pocket. From the pocket's bottom stared the man's eye.

"You naughty boy," scolded the father impulsively. "What on earth got into you?"

"I was going to show my science teacher," explained the son, his bottom lip quivering.

"Oh. Well . . . well that was a nice thought." He would have walked on, but the eye held him. He reprimanded his son, but calmly this time. "Son, we must think of the poor mortician. He can't make the man look nice without the eye, can he? You must bring it back."

The boy's eyes blinked rapidly, but he did not answer.

"Go on," insisted the father, nudging his son. He began to worry that this demand of his might some day be ferreted out by some psychoanalyst, and he blushed as he imagined the accusing finger pointed at him. He knew it was old-fashioned to be so demanding, but he reiterated his command. "Bring it back to where you got it, son."

The boy took two reluctant steps back, then pitched the eyeball as he had seen his father pitch horseshoes. The eyeball landed right on target. "Nice. . ." began the father. "Nice boy," he completed. The form and the footwork had been exemplary. He reached to pat his son's back, but grasped the sticky, outstretched hand instead. He turned quickly then, and was surprised by a tall, slightly disheveled man, his shoelaces still loose, just a few paces away.

"Did you hear a shot around here a little bit ago?" inquired the tall man nonchalantly. "The wife said she heard a shot. . ."

"Yes, a man's been shot. Right down there," broke in the father, pointing. "Half his face is blown off. I'm just going to call a mortician now." The father and son walked on then, as the newcomer went to inspect the body.

"It's Williger!" he gulped, seeing in his mind the fence that separated their lots. He felt for a pulse.

"Hey!" he yelled. The father and son, a long way off now, stopped. "Better make that an ambulance. He's still got a pulse." The father nodded as though he heard.

Kneeling beside Williger, the tall man remembered the conversation of a few days ago. "Yeah, Williger," he had said, "I suppose before long you'll have to be moving out of your house and into a rest home. And they cost money," he had warned, remembering the estates he had handled as a lawyer. "I suppose you'll have to sell your house and lot to pay for that." He had not given him an offer, in deference to Williger's feelings.

Now, however, seeing Williger's blood-matted hair, his mangled face, he even remembered what he was going to offer him. "My neighbor," he said aloud suddenly, but was embarrassed when he heared his own voice. He looked sheepishly around to see if anyone else had heard, but he saw no one. Williger's loud "No rest home for me" came back to him now. "No, Williger," he said comfortingly, "I guess you won't have to waste away in a rest home after all." He took hold of the wrist again to feel for a pulse. The limp hand felt heavy as he lifted the wrist.

Suddenly the tall man felt a tap on his shoulder. He spun around so quickly that he nearly skinned his nose on a badge which a man was concealing in the palm of his left hand. In his right hand he held a pad and pen. He wore a plain brown suit topped by a small-rimmed hat pushed firmly down onto his forehead.

"Special Investigator," he said almost inaudibly.

"Oh," murmured the tall neighbor meekly, still kneeling.

"You've a constitutional right to say nothing if you don't want to," said the Investigator politely, holding his pen to his pad. "But," he added with a seductive smile, "would you like to confess?"

"Oh, no, you've got this all wrong," replied the neighbor. "I just came here. Wife thought she heard a shot or firecracker so I came out to look." He noticed his own loose shoelaces at this point and started to tie them. The Investigator's hand was scribbling furiously. Finally, he looked up. "Care to tell me what you saw?" he purred.

The neighbor, still on one knee, stopped tying his shoes. "Well, sure. Saw a man and his son coming away from Williger here." He motioned with his head. "I asked them if they'd heard a shot." The Investigator started to write, but stopped.

"Did you inform them of their right not to answer you?" he asked.

"Well, no, don't believe I did," replied the neighbor. He started to tie his shoe again.

"I was afraid so," remarked the Investigator. He began to erase.

Just then another man walked up. He was pointing impressively to a patch on his sleeve while still ten yards away.

"Park Director," he informed them. "This man must be moved immediately." He eyed the Investigator quizzically. "If you don't mind, sir, I don't want this accident to have happened in my park."

"Oh, I see," said the Investigator meekly, erasing furiously. "Where shall it have happened?"

"How about on the sidewalk just off the park," suggested the Park Director, taking hold of Williger's leg to drag him to the sidewalk.

"Can't you wait?" asked the neighbor, vaguely uneasy. "I think an ambulance is coming now. I hear a siren."

"Well, I suppose," said the Park Director, sulking. "Just don't want anyone to think it happened in my park." He walked over to Williger's head and began covering the blood-stained sand with clean sand. He toiled silently, landscaping first with the side of one foot and then with the side of the other. The Investigator walked over to protest, but after observing for a moment, he said, "My son should be here. He has a toy bulldozer."

The keening wail of the siren stirred the neighbor's thinking. Something in him wanted to help put Williger onto a stretcher. "Yes. I helped put old man Williger on a stretcher, helped toss him on the wagon yet," he would recount for his golfing partners tomorrow. "Told them to take good care of him, and if he couldn't pay, I would." He imagined himself saying this, saying it because he knew that he *wouldn't* have to pay. But he feared that his golfing partners might not comprehend his subtlety. They might say as he approached them later, "There's a guy who'd give you the shirt off his back." He could not bear such humiliation. He would have to laugh loudly when he said it to his golfing partners, if he said it at all.

In a moment the ambulance swooped in. A driver and another male nurse's aide, both dressed in white, tumbled out. A couple of small boys came shuffling up from the other direction at the same time. The Investigator wrote down the license number of the ambulance. The Park Director accosted the ambulance driver. He tapped his shoulder patch ominously. "Remember, Bud, it's illegal to drive a motor vehicle on city playgrounds, so don't forget that you picked up your cargo *outside* of this playground, not *in* it." The aid rolled out the stretcher. The neighbor was about to speak. "Doc," he was going to say, "this man's been shot." He was waiting for the aid to look at him.

"Move aside, Mister," said the aid. The neighbor hopscotched over. As the aid placed the stretcher beside Williger, the two boys nosed in, one moving to the head, the other to the feet.

"I took his pulse," the neighbor said finally.

The Investigator was still writing furiously. The Park Director was stockpiling sand between his feet in anticipation of their moving Williger. The two men in white moved silently beside the body.

"Now, let's the three of us lift him," said the driver. The neighbor, the aid, and the driver knelt beside Williger. "Now when we lift him, you boys each shove your end of the stretcher under him, instructed the driver. The boys looked at each other, and each took hold of an end with one eye on the other. "All set?"

asked the driver. Then to the men beside him he said, "Ready, lift."

No sooner had they raised the limp Williger than several coins fell out of his pocket. Both boys let go of the stretcher and dove under the uplifted body. Their arms and legs threshed about as they wrestled underneath Williger for his coins.

"Oh no you don't." "It's mine." "Give it here." "You dog!" "Ouch!" The Investigator was on his haunches nearby measuring the distance from Williger to the nearest tree. The Park Director was hastily shoving clean sand over the red-stained sand underneath Williger's uplifted head. Suddenly the one boy rolled out and took off like a rabbit out of the brush, hotly pursued by the other. The three men, straining to maintain their balance, still held Williger on their outstretched forearms.

"Those kids show real promise," observed the driver. He looked at the stretcher a few yards away. He considered the Park Director with the sand between his feet, and the Investigator on his haunches. Then to the aide and the neighbor beside him he said, "Let's try making it to the stretcher." They walked like three penguins to an altar, then bowed Williger onto the stretcher. The neighbor was thinking how he would be saying tomorrow, "My arms nearly broke off. He must have weighed two-hundred-and-twenty pounds."

They had just hoisted the stretcher into the ambulance when the mortician arrived.

"Hey, stealing my customer?" he asked. He hopped into the rear door of the ambulance before the aid could close it and huddled by the body of Williger. The driver started the engine while his aid slammed the door with the mortician inside. The neighbor was thinking of saying, "Remember, if you need any help, just call on me," but he wasn't sure his boisterous laugh would allay their accusing glances. The Investigator was measuring the height of the wet spot on the tree, computing the size of the dog who had stopped by. The Park Director stood duck-footed, with little mounds of sand inside the arch of each foot, ready to cover the tracks of the ambulance.

Just as the ambulance began to move, the mortician shouted with glee. "Wait! Wait! Open the chute! He's dead! He's mine!

Stop the buggy! I'll back my wagon by."

The Park Director sprinted to the driver's window. "Don't you stop until you're off this park or I'll give you a summons! Do your switching on the road." The Investigator heaved an audible sigh. Homicide could take over the case now. He ripped several sheets of paper from his pad and pitched them to the wind. The neighbor was calculating the value of Williger's property when he heard the mortician's shout. He reached up and caught one of the floating sheets of the Investigator to do some figuring as he followed the ambulance to the hearse. He thought of how tomorrow he would be saying, "Yeah, I helped dump poor old Williger out of the ambulance into the hearse."

Williger evaporated behind the closed doors of the sleek hearse.

The zealous mortician took on the last burden—molding the lump of clay before him into an effective advertisement for Don's Funeral Parlor. But only the neighbor peeked in to see it. When he did, the strains of "I'm Always Chasing Rainbows" caressed the garnished coffin. He whistled the tune over and over the next day as he golfed.

Questions for Reflection and Discussion:

1. Which bystander is most like the Samaritan in our Lord's parable?
2. What prevents each character from being a truly good Samaritan?
3. What satiric observations on contemporary secular education are dramatically presented?
4. How are all the (living) characters alike?
5. What does the parable suggest about the treatment of the aged?
6. How is the imagery of "blood" and "sand" used in this story?

JOSEPH BAYLY

I Saw Gooley Fly

Until Herb Gooley stepped out of his third-floor dorm window and flew away into the wild blue yonder, he was just an ordinary sort of guy.

But I'm getting ahead of my story.

I first met Gooley in that little hamburger and malt joint just off campus—Pete's Place. I'd never have noticed the guy except that he dropped a mustard bottle, and the stuff squirted down the front of his storm jacket. Now, I'm a sophomore at the time and this guy's a frosh. (No mistaking them, during those early weeks of the quarter.) But he's making such a mess out of wiping the stuff off that I help him. Brother, what a mess. But Herb was the sort of fellow who could hardly wipe his nose himself, let alone the mustard.

When he had the stuff pretty well wiped off his coat and shirt (you could still see those bright yellow streaks), I ask him where he sacks out.

"Pollard," he says.

"That hole. Must be a frosh, huh? You'll learn. 'Course you can transfer after a quarter. Me, I'm at Sigma Phi House. Know the place that looks like a country club over on Lincoln?"

He doesn't know it. So we pay Pete and walk out. That is, I walk out. Herb falls over a cigarette machine that stands near the door.

Next time I notice the guy is at Homecoming.

It's during the frosh-soph tug of war. (They really had pressure on those fire hoses that year.) We're ready for the final pull and the gun goes off. Suddenly the whole frosh team's yelling to stop pulling. So, after they turn the hoses on us, we stop; and here's Gooley, looking sort of dazed, with the rope twisted clear around his arm. I'll never know how he did it. They get it off and take him to the infirmary. Nothing broken, but he sure must have had a painful arm for a few days.

I remember—sometime the following fall—seeing a crowd gathered around the front of Hinton's department store. So I pull over to the curb, and here is the college station wagon half-in, half-out of Hinton's show window. What a scene! Bodies all over the place, one of them broken in two across the hood. Gooley's standing there holding a head.

Maybe losing his driving privileges for awhile got him interested in flying. At any rate he comes back from Christmas vacation his junior year able to fly. Able to actually fly, mind you, not just able to fly a plane.

His roommate (Jerry Watson, it was) told us about it the next day. Seems Gooley had been studying late, and finally he turns the book over, switches off his desk light and says, "Think I'll go down to Pete's for a malted."

"Too late," Jerry says. "It's three minutes to twelve and he closes at midnight."

"I'll fly down." Gooley says it matter-of-factly, just like he's saying he'll run or something.

So over to the window he goes (Jerry all the while thinking Gooley is suddenly developing a sense of humor), lifts it up, and steps off the ledge.

Their room is on the third floor.

Jerry waits a second for the thud, then dashes into the hall and down the stairs yelling, "Gooley fell out the window! Somebody call a doctor!"

No Gooley on the ground, or anywhere around. So they think Jerry's pulling their leg.

"Honest, fellows, Gooley stepped out of our window. Said he'd fly down to Pete's. Honest he did."

So they wait around for Gooley to come back and, when he does, they start firing questions.

"Sure I can fly. Jerry was telling you the straight stuff. Here, I'll show you." And with that he takes off into the wild blue yonder.

None of us believed the story when we heard it. Would you? In the first place, people can ride bicycles, people can row boats, people can fly planes even, but nobody can fly.

In the second place, if anybody could fly, Herb Gooley wouldn't be the man. That guy couldn't even walk.

It began to snow about supper time the next day and it snowed all through the night. Next morning the ground is covered, but some of the walks are shoveled off. I'm walking down the cleared path at the quad when I notice something. Fresh footprints go out on the snow a few yards, then there's nothing. Nothing. No trampled snow, no feet turning around. Just footprints going out and stopping.

Within a few days nobody needs any more circumstantial evidence. We've all seen it—Gooley flying.

He'd be walking along with you and, suddenly, he's airborne. Nothing spectacular. I mean it was all very quiet. His rise was almost vertical, and he flew along at about fifteen or twenty miles per hour. Just above the treetops. He'd sort of bank to turn.

That winter and spring you should have seen Gooley come into class on the third or fourth floor of Old Main. Brother, that was a sight to behold. It got to be a regular custom to open the window just before the bell. I'll never forget the day we had a visiting lecturer. Nobody had told him.

Let me tell you there was a run on the library for books on aero-dynamics, aircraft design and any other subject that even faintly bears on flying. Guys were spending all their free time soaking up all they could learn. So were most of the girls.

I don't want you to get the idea that we talked a lot about it. Nobody would admit that he wanted to fly, but most everybody did. Nothing in the world I wanted more. (Seems sort of funny now.)

The college flying course tripled in size. (Flying planes, that is—but it was as close as we could come to personal flight.) In bull sessions we talked into the small hours about how Gooley probably did it.

You see, Gooley wasn't saying.

Of course, later there was some reaction—a lot of people began to call Gooley a freak. It sort of made us laugh, though, when one of the most outspoken anti-Gooleyites was found with a brain concussion at the foot of the Old Zach monument. (He got over it all right.)

I think the college administration was sort of ashamed to have Gooley as a student. So they bring in this guy Sevorsky for a special lecture series called "Flight Emphasis Week." Brother, were those lectures packed out. Standing room only.

Halfway through the week we realize that Sevorsky can't fly. We're standing outside Old Main, waiting for him to leave the President's office, which is on the second floor. So how does he come down? Why, he walks down the stairs and out the front door. This guy can design airplanes, we say; he has the latest scoop on jets and helicopters; but he can't fly.

About a dozen students show up for his final lecture.

Most of us had heard a myth about some ancient Greek who could fly until he got too near the sun. So we think maybe there's a clue. Interest switches to books on ancient Greek mythology, and the library puts them on the reserve shelf.

You know, I've always been surprised that Gooley didn't tell us how to do it, or at least how *he* did it. He couldn't help knowing how interested we all were. But he kept his mouth shut. So none of us learned to fly.

It's a funny thing, but I still have a sense of loss at not learning Gooley's secret. And other grads have confessed the same thing to me.

What happened to Gooley? I've often wondered about that. He transferred that fall to another college where, they say, all the students know how to fly.

Questions for Reflection and Discussion:

1. What does flying represent in this story?
2. Explain "books on aerodynamics" and "the college flying course."

3. How does Bayly use irony in his presentation of Sevorsky and "Flight Emphasis Week"?
4. Evaluate Gooley's close-mouthed policy in terms of the meaning of the parable.
5. What kind of college is the setting of the story?
6. What is the ironic meaning of the statement "If anybody could fly, Herb Gooley wouldn't be the man"?

JOSEPH BAYLY

Ceiling Zero

My roomate is a guy named Gooley. Herb Gooley.

He transferred to this crummy little school in the boondocks about six months ago. When he first arrived, we were all asking why he left a big, well-known college at the beginning of his senior year. Everybody's heard of it; nobody's heard of us.

Only thing we have that they don't have is a flight school. What they have and we don't have would fill a book.

One night I ask Herb straight out, "Why did you come here?"

"One reason," he says. "Last Christmas vacation I learned to fly. So I decided to switch to a flight school, a place where everyone could fly. That's why I'm here."

I should explain that I don't mean flying planes, or gliders, or balloons, or anything. I mean we can fly, period.

We can step out of a window and be airborne. I remember my first flight—it was while I was still in high school—off a barn in the Blue Ridge Mountains. Some of the guys and girls here have been flying every siince they were little kids.

So the reason Herb Gooley gave for coming here made sense. Except for one thing, which he couldn't have known before he came. It's the sort of thing you don't learn from a catalog.

Gooley is a sensitive guy—withdrawn. Doesn't talk to many people. But there's some reason for being as he is: for one thing, he got off to a bad start.

I've never seen a happier freshman than Gooley, when he first showed up. I don't mean that he was actually a freshman—like I said, he was a transfer senior. But he had that same stupid innocence.

One of those hot afternoons in September—like so many days when school has just begun—I was stripped to the waist, arranging my clothes on hangers, when this new student comes through the window. He flew in—our room is on the third floor of Derwin Hall.

"I'm Herb Gooley," he says. "Boy, have I ever been looking forward to coming here."

"To this crummy school? Why?" I ask.

He looks sort of surprised. "Why, because it's a flight school. You can fly, can't you? The other guys in this dorm can fly, can't they? And the girls—just think of having a flying date. Wow!"

Should I tell him straight off, or should I let him find out for himself?

I guess I'm sort of chicken, because I decide not to say anything. Let someone else tell him.

"Yeah, this is a flight school, all right. We can all fly, including the profs—and the administration. You can have that bed over there by the door, Gooley. And that dresser, and either closet, except that I've got my things in this one. The public relations department can fly, too. They prepare the catalog."

He doesn't say anything, but begins to unpack. First thing out of his suitcase is a copy of Aerodynamic Theory. It goes on his desk.

Around five-thirty I head for the dining hall. "Coming along?" I ask.

"Not yet," Gooley says. "Don't wait for me. I want to finish here first. I'll be along before it closes."

So I walk on over and go through the cafeteria line. I find my crowd and sit down to eat with them.

We're on dessert, when there's a little stir over by the door.

"What do we have here?" someone asks.

"An exhibitionist."

"A new student, you can tell that. Nobody else would fly on

campus."

Sure enough—it's Herb Gooley, my new roommate. He comes through the door and touches down gently, by the stack of trays and the silver holder. He's got a smooth technique.

Everybody gets sort of quiet. I don't know about the others, but suddenly I'm thinking about some of my flights in high-school days.

"You're too late," this battle-ax who runs the cafeteria says. "We close at six-thirty. She's absolutely right, which is what she always is.

"Serves him right," a girl going back for seconds on iced tea says, loud enough for Herb to hear. "He's just a showoff."

Gooley looks sort of hurt, but he doesn't say anything, either to battle-ax or to battle-ax, j.g. He just heads out the door. Walking.

"He'll learn," someone at my table says. "We all learned."

And he did, during the next few weeks.

First thing he finds out is that here nobody flies. In spite of this being a flight school, and everyone can fly—theoretically, we're all grounded.

There's a lot of talk about flight, of course. Flight courses, references to flight in a lot of other courses, a daily flight hour. But nobody flies.

Some of us came here planning to be flight instructors. I myself wanted to teach Africans how to fly, but that didn't last long.

Actually, the deadest things are the flight courses. They use Aerodynamic Theory as the text, but you'd never recognize it. One flight out of a hayloft has more excitement to it than a year of that course.

One night we get into a discussion on our floor of the dorm.

"Look, Gooley," one of the guys says, "tell us about the college you were in before you came here. Is it true that they have more exciting courses than we do here?"

"A lot of them, yes," Gooley says. "But they don't know anything about how to fly."

"Are the girls there real swingers?"

"I guess so. But they can't fly."

The way Herb answers sort of frustrates the guys who are asking the questions, because they would jump at a chance to transfer to the school he came from.

"I think this flying isn't all it's cracked up to be," one of them says.

"I feel the same way," another chimes in. "And besides, it seems sort of selfish to me to fly when the rest of the world is walking."

"Not only selfish—to them you look like some kind of a nut, up there above the ground. From here on in, any flights I take are going to be when there's nobody around to see me."

"Besides, the world needs to be taught how to walk. And pavements and roads need to be improved."

"Did any of you read John Robin's book? It's a pretty strong critique of Aerodynamic Theory, and he does an effective job of questioning the usual foundations of flight. The significant thing is that Robin is a flyer, not a walker."

That was the only time I ever heard Herb Gooley swear. Then he stomps across the room and dives out the window. (It is a cold night, but fortunately we had opened the window because the room was getting stuffy. If we hadn't, I think Herb would have gone right through the glass.)

He didn't return until early next morning. I heard him at the window and got up to open it. It had begun to snow, and he was covered. He looked nearly exhausted, but happier than I'd seen him since the day he first arrived.

That night marked a change in Herb Gooley, a change that came to affect the whole school. Only, I didn't know it at the time.

He began to fly again. On campus.

Now when you're with flyers, flying isn't remarkable—actually it's the basic minimum, it's taken for granted. What worries us is perfection, and it's sort of embarrassing—around other flyers—to try an extra little maneuver, or to stay aloft longer than usual. There can be such a letdown. And the competition is so keen. There's always someone who can fly better than you.

That's the reason nobody flies here. At least they didn't, not until Gooley took it up again.

Like the flight prof says, "This is a school for flying, not an airport. You've come here to learn more about flying, not to fly. We want to teach you how to fly with real conviction." Then he draws diagrams on the blackboard. And he walks across the campus.

Meanwhile, Herb is getting better and better. I mean his flying is improving. You can see him on a moonlit night, trying all sorts of flight gymnastics.

Moonlit nights. That brings me to another side of the change in Gooley.

He began to have flying dates. Not many—none of the girls, except one or two, would be caught dead on a flight date, especially with Herb.

What can you talk about on a flying date? What can you do? I ask you.

We discuss it while Gooley's out of the dorm. He's out a lot those last months of school. Not just flying or on flight dates, but teaching a bunch of kids to fly at the community center in town, studying Aerodynamic Theory with a little group of students. The guys can't understand why Herb keeps at it.

"Sure we can fly—at least as well as that guy Gooley. But after all, real life is down here on the earth. It's not as if we were birds."

"Besides, we've got to learn to relate to the walkers. And that's a lot harder to do than flying."

"I've found—I don't know about the rest of you guys—but I've found that they're not much interested in my flying ability. I mean, the walkers aren't. So it's important to show them that I can walk."

"Don't get me wrong, it's not that I'm against flying. I'm not. But you don't have to fly to be for flying."

So the year ends.

We graduate.

I ask Gooley, while we're packing, what he plans to do next year.

"Grad school," he says. "In a walking university. You see, I was reading Aerodynamic Theory the other day, where it says that you can take off best against the wind."

Questions for Reflection and Discussion:

1. What kind of college is the setting of this story?
2. Explain the attitude of the students towards flying.
3. What is "a copy of Aerodynamic Theory"?
4. In what way are the references to teaching people to walk and to improving roads meant satirically?
5. Evaluate Gooley's choice of grad school at a walking university.
6. What techniques does the author use to make the dialogue sound realistic?